**Structure and performance
in adult education**

Structure and performance
in adult education

Graham Mee
Harold Wiltshire

Longman
London and New York

Longman Group Limited London

*Associated companies, branches and representatives
throughout the world*

*Published in the United States of America
by Longman Inc., New York*

© Longman Group Limited 1978

First published 1978

Library of Congress Cataloging in Publication Data

Wiltshire, Harold.
   Structure and performance in adult education.

   1. Adult education.   I. Mee, Graham, joint author.
II. Title.
LC5215.W53   334   77-7051
ISBN 0-582-48944-X

Type photoset in 10 point Times by Woolaston Parker Ltd, Leicester
Printed in Great Britain by
Richard Clay (The Chaucer Press) Ltd, Bungay, Suffolk

Contents

Foreword

By 'adult education' we mean publicly provided education addressed primarily to adults and mainly serving other than vocational needs. We are concerned only with the adult education provided by the Local Education Authorities in England and Wales, not with that provided by the Responsible Bodies. This narrow focus has meant that when we were looking, for example, at multi-purpose institutions or organisations it has been only with the adult education aspect of their work that we have been concerned and it is upon this alone that we have felt competent to comment. We have throughout written 'he' and 'his' when we should have written 'he or she' or 'his or her', feeling that the interests of simplicity and euphony took precedence over those of sex equality. Regrettably, the masculine pronoun is the correct one in far too many cases.

We started out two and a half years ago intending (in the words of our original submission to the Department of Education and Science) to 'describe, analyse and classify' organisational and institutional patterns, to 'relate these to the growing body of organisational theory' and to make some 'appraisal of their various virtues and defects'. We cannot claim to have wholly succeeded. Probably the task was in any case beyond the powers of a research team which consisted of two people, one part-time throughout the whole period and one spare-time for a year and a half and full-time for a year. But as we visited more institutions, talked with more people and became more familiar with our material we began to see the task differently: institutions seemed more various, more complex and more resistant to classification and quantitative analysis than we had imagined – and organisational theory did not seem to be of as much direct help as we had expected. Without conscious direction we found our interests shifting somewhat from institutions to the people who worked in them, so that this report has turned out to be at least as much about adult educators as about institutions and organisations. On balance we do not regret this.

None of this would have been possible without the support of the Department of Education and Science, which has financed the whole enterprise although it is, of course, in no way responsible for the views expressed. We want to record our gratitude to the Department and to the many busy people upon whose expertise and patience we have drawn and who have given their help and advice so willingly: officers of the Department of Education and Science and of Local Education Authorities, Her Majesty's Inspectors (in particuler Mr Konrad Elsdon), University colleagues, and of course our fellow adult educators up and down the country. A thank you also to our wives; being married to an adult educator makes its own special demands – additionally they have cheerfully tolerated the absences and unsociable hours of the researcher.

Many things about the present plight of adult education seem to us profoundly depressing and discouraging, but our encounters with adult educators tended always to cheer us up for they seemed to us to face their manifold difficulties with commitment, courage and resourcefulness. We have tried to understand and to interpret their problems and their aspirations; we hope that we have done so fairly and that what we have written may be of use to them.

Graham Mee
Harold Wiltshire
March 1977

Chapter 1

The administrative context of adult education

Adult education is part of the complex and haphazard structure of publicly provided post-school education in England and Wales. This is an attempt to indicate its place in that structure.

1. Publicly provided post-school education falls into two main sectors called (unhelpfully) Higher and Further Education. Higher Education is the business of such institutions as Universities, Polytechnics, Colleges of Education, Colleges of Higher Education and the like; it provides courses at degree or similar level. These institutions are financed by direct or indirect grant from the Department of Education and Science and/or by grant from the Local Education Authority. They tend to claim a considerable degree of autonomy and to concentrate upon full-time courses.

2. Further Education is a much more complex field comprising a great variety of institutions and an enormous range of courses, mostly at lower academic levels and mostly part-time. The institutions in this sector are financed and controlled by Local Education Authorities. The amount and the nature of Further Education provision can vary very widely between one authority and another. It has grown and changed rapidly in the last few decades and is still growing and changing. Further Education falls into two main, though ill-defined, subsections:
(a) a mainly work-related or vocational sector comprising a great variety of mainly part-time courses leading to examinations and to technical, professional and occupational qualifications and addressed primarily to the 16–19 age group;
(b) a mainly leisure-related or non-vocational sector also comprising a great variety of mainly part-time courses not directed towards examinations or qualifications and addressed to adults.

3. Non-vocational Further Education itself falls into two main subsections:
(a) Youth service, addressed mainly to the 14–20 age group but in fact most active at the younger end of that age band;
(b) Adult education, addressed to adults in general with no strictly applied age limits; students may be 16 or 90, but their modal age tends to be somewhere in the 30s.

4. The Education Act of 1944 lays upon Local Education Authorities the responsibility for providing, or securing the provision of, adult education and most of it (perhaps seven-eighths) is in fact directly provided by them as part of their programme of Further Education. But a small amount (perhaps one-eighth) is provided through what are called the Responsible Bodies – mainly the districts of the Workers' Educational Association and the extramural (or similar) departments of the Universities. This work has links with Higher Education as well as Further Education and is grant-aided directly by the Department of Education and Science. It makes a small but distinctive contribution, mainly in the cognitive studies (other than languages), and has to be taken into account in any survey of adult education as a whole since many Local Education Authorities restrict their own provision in the cognitive field in the expectation that the Responsible Bodies will fill the gap.

5. There is a problem of nomenclature. 'Non-vocational Further Education' is cumbersome, and Local Education Authorities tend to describe all this work as 'recreational' – a handy term, but one which can cause misunderstandings and which sometimes seems to devalue what it describes. We prefer, and have used throughout, the term 'adult education' which is simple, carries no overtones, indicates the relevant age group, has been in use for a very long time and is, as we have found, generally understood throughout England and Wales.

6. Within each Local Education Authority the structure through which adult education is administered may differ. At one extreme, the responsibility may rest with an assistant director of education who will have a substantial time commitment to adult education within a broader Further Education remit. Such an appointment at this level will usually be supported by a specialist adult education appointment at the next level and by one or more advisers or inspectors. At the other extreme we may find an authority with no full-time adult educator at all in its headquarters staff but perhaps with one lone organiser whose status and salary may be no higher than, or even below that, of a head of centre in another authority.

    Whatever the staffing pattern, the senior adult educator will typically report directly or indirectly to the Further Education Sub-Committee of the Education Committee, although there are a very few authorities in which adult education is seen as part of leisure services and the competent committee then becomes (it is variously named) Leisure or Recreation.

7. There may be an additional level of responsibility interposed between the head of centre and county or city hall in the person of an area or divisional officer who has a general responsibility for education in that area but who tends, inevitably, to be mainly concerned with

schools. The lines of authority and responsibility between a head of centre and (*a*) such a non-specialist area officer, (*b*) a specialist officer at headquarters – and, in the case of multi-purpose institutions, (*c*) a headmaster or principal – tend to be ill-defined and unsatisfactory.

8. The regulatory frameworks within which adult education works also vary widely between authorities which exercise a hierarchic control and those which emphasise the autonomy of the individual centre. On the one hand there may be an allocation of a fixed, itemised budget with no possibility of virement, fees and enrolment requirements all determined centrally and the head of centre having virtually no discretionary powers. On the other hand the head of centre may have control over the spending of his budget and over fees and enrolment requirements provided that a certain minimum income is produced overall and a certain average enrolment is maintained over the whole programme.

9. Our concern throughout will be with adult education at the level of the centre, and we shall try to look at it through the eyes of those who have to plan and maintain centre programmes. From this point of view the total structure within which adult education works seems confusing and often unhelpful, and the administrative frameworks set up by the Local Education Authorities will in some places seem to be enabling and supportive and in others to be restrictive and discouraging. And from this point of view the differences between authorities – far greater than those in the vocational sector of Further Education – must seem enormous and quite irrational.

Chapter 2

Sources of evidence and their treatment

Our methodology is qualitative rather than quantitative, reflecting in the main our own inclinations but also the difficulties of quantification in this area; there are no firm bases for sampling since there are no reliable national data on numbers of institutions, students or courses. Hence an early decision was taken that whatever other investigatory tools were used our prime source of information would be lengthy interviews with adult educators at centre level. So, therefore, we have studied the institutions and their functioning through the eyes of the organisers of programmes and not through the eyes of teachers or students; to have done so would have trebled the life of the project. Further research could well focus on the teachers' and students' perceptions and experience of adult education organisations.

The reliance on recorded interviews has been qualified by an awareness of the distinction between words and deeds. Thus we have sought to check interviewees' statements by also analysing their programmes. We have used quantitative methods where they seemed appropriate and where the nature of the evidence permitted them to be used but with a realisation of their limitations for we accept the contention that it is in 'the interrelationship and interdependence of quantitative and qualitative methodology' that the 'understanding (of) the complexities of human behaviour'[1] lies.

We have been greatly helped by the opportunity, which we have enjoyed over many years, of working with Local Education Authorities' adult educators on the University of Nottingham's Diploma and Master's courses, on summer schools and in conferences and meetings; without this we should have been much slower in developing an understanding of the problems which adult educators face and the attitudes and values that they bring to them. This experience meant that we started our research with certain broadly based assumptions in mind: that there would be marked differences in the programmes of different institutions and significant variations in the work experience and role conceptions of those working in them; that adult education is a developing service which has to be flexible in response to emerging and changing needs and that different types of institution would vary in their ability to respond, that is in their capacity to innovate. Our task was to test for these and any other differences, to quantify them where possible, to analyse them and to try to account for them.

There was no preconceived theoretical framework within which we would try to account for what we found; this has been developed as the research proceeded. Our objective was to achieve understanding through the use of whatever data collection techniques seemed appropriate. The approach in several ways reflects the 'theoretical sampling' methodology advocated by Glaser and Strauss: 'Theoretical sampling is the process of data collection for generating theory whereby the analyst jointly collects, codes, and analyses his data and decides what data to collect next and where to find them, in order to develop his theory as it emerges. This process of data collection is controlled by the emerging theory. . . .'[2]

Initially local authorities were asked to provide information about their adult education service and were given limited guidance on what might be useful. Although a few authorities sent copious material, most, though expressing a willingness to help, had little or no material readily available and asked for specific queries; the resulting questions also evoked a very varied response. At this stage we were left with both a strong impression and also a problem; many authorities did not appear to know much about and were perhaps not very interested in their adult education service; how were we to obtain the information which had not been forthcoming? It was decided that a questionnaire addressed to all those practitioners with responsibility for a programme of classes might enable us to close the gaps in our knowledge. Additionally it could be used as a guide in the design of interview schedules and would suggest approaches and hypotheses to be tried out in interviews.

Recently it has been advocated that in adult education we should not allow 'head counting surveys . . . to become the major research activity'; the researcher is further exhorted to 'triangulate' or use several methods simultaneously.[3] We were doubtful of the value of head counting. Though we were not conscious of being involved in the process of 'triangulating' we decided to utilise the range of investigatory tools detailed below because they served our purposes; as the data converged or diverged so our 'theory' emerged. It is comforting to know, however, that others support what seemed to us a common-sense way of tackling a largely unresearched area.

The main investigatory tools used were:
1. Collection of data from local authorities;
2. Questionnaire;
3. Programme analysis;
4. Interviews;
5. Diary.

1. Data collection from local authorities

Directors of Education were asked for information under the following headings:
• The general pattern of organisation and finance;

- The organisation and financing of individual institutions;
- Staffing (full-time and part-time);
- Students and fee structures;
- Programmes and patterns of provision (for the area as a whole or for individual institutions).

A further letter, sent in December 1976, asked for details of enrolments for the years 1974–76, expenditure cuts and changes in regulations for 1976–77.

2. Questionnaire

The questionnaire was sent through Directors of Education to all heads of centre (the term 'centre' being used as a convenient shorthand term to cover every kind of institution that provices a regular programme, large or small, centralised or scattered, of non-vocational adult education classes – e.g. Evening Institutes, Adult Education Centres, Community Centres, adult education sectors of Community Schools and Colleges, departments responsible for adult education in Colleges of Further Education, etc.).

Respondents forwarded their replies directly to the research office using a prepaid label. The response of some 1,500 returns exceeded expectations. Given the lack of any firm statistical base it is not possible to determine what percentage of the total number of heads of centre this represented. However, it is probable that the returns covered well over one-third of the national adult education programme.

The size of the 'sample' was not, however, of any great concern because the replies were to be used in conjuction with other tools, particularly the interviews, designed to check the information given. Critically, it filled in many of the gaps left by the partial failure of our initial enquiry to local authorities.

Information sought:
- location of centre;
- job title; full-time, joint- or spare-time;
- staff employed;
- availability of premises;
- enrolment;
- influence of others on the programme;
- influence of method of financing a programme;
- problems encountered;
- developments;
- functions of adult education.

3. Programme analysis 1975–76

The whole of the work of an institution is not of course displayed in its published programme, but the greater part of it is, and when we checked evidence from programmes against that from other sources it became clear that programmes are a much more reliable guide to the nature and range of an institution's work than is sometimes maintained. However, we added questions to our interview schedules specifically designed to fill in gaps in the evidence from programmes.

Courses announced in programmes were classified into four main and six subsidiary subject categories; these are described and discussed in Chapter 5. In addition to this we analysed programmes for evidence of innovative tendencies and derived from this analysis five 'indices' of innovative capacity; these are described and discussed in Chapter 7.

The programmes analysed fall into two main groups. The Survey group consists of those of the institutions in which interviews were conducted plus those of institutions of a similar type within the same authority. This gave a total of 22,761 courses. A Crosscheck group was drawn from ten authorities not included in the twenty-six of the Survey group, but similarly scattered geographically. This added another 11,607 courses.

4. Interviews

As already indicated, interviews with heads of centre were always intended to be the main part of the whole enterprise. There were three main reasons for this: first, we wanted to try to see organisations and institutions through the eyes of those who work in them; second, the degree of autonomy in adult education institutions is often so great that each one can become – and has to be treated as – a special case; third, an adult education institution is, in general, small enough for one man to have a decisive influence upon its work.

A major difficulty lay in determining which authorities to visit. Initially we took the advice of experienced colleagues with a wide acquaintance with adult education nationally; they identified what they felt were particularly interesting and characteristic examples of different types of organisation. In consequence, we set out initially to visit those authorities whose adult education was based on a particular type of organisation.

This early round of visits, combined with the analysis of the questionnaire, identified questions which suggested other visits. Thus the range of influences determining the programme of visits was varied and complex but increasingly, as they developed, the visits were determined by the need to answer a narrowing band of specific questions, that is by our emerging 'theory'.

In all we visited twenty-six authorities. The interviews were conducted primarily within institutions, though where more information was needed about an authority's structure and policy the senior officer responsible was also interviewed. Within institutions attention concentrated primarily on those with a direct responsibility for planning and maintaining a programme of adult education (i.e. 'heads of centre') and secondarily, in colleges and schools, with principals/

wardens. The number of interviews was as follows:

'heads of centre'   105 (including pilot study to test schedule)
principals/wardens   40
senior officers   16

The result of this interviewing programme was a body of testimony, mainly from practitioners, amounting to over one million words.

In total, interviews were conducted in more than twenty institutions in each of the following categories: Specialised Institutions with full-time staff, Specialised Institutions with spare-time staff, Community Schools, and Colleges of Further Education. There were fewer interviews in institutions in authorities in which adult education is based on a joint adult and youth service and also where it is located outside of the education service altogether in a recreation and leisure services department (see Ch. 4 for a detailed typology of institutions). Although we visited some Community Centres in the early stages of the enquiry and received many questionnaire replies from them it quickly became apparent that they would have to be excluded given the time and resources available.

It can be argued that the interview sample is in some cases too small to be of value. However, the interviews have to be taken together with the other tools used; they have, for example, been used as a check on hypotheses generated by the questionnaire and in turn have been checked through programme analysis. Evidence from any one source may be inconclusive, but collectively the investigatory tools have produced a large body of data and it is where evidence from these different sources converges that we can be confident of the findings.

Interview schedules were used in order to ensure that certain basic information was elicited and to provide some measure of consistency between interviews. But the schedules were not detailed, and the interviews were lengthy (normally about one and half hours), so that we were able to put supplementary questions and the interviewee was able to talk at length about matters which were of interest to him. These conversations – for that is what they became – were all recorded and the recordings transcribed so that we could read and analyse them at leisure.

5. Diary

The simple diary which our head of centre interviewees were asked to keep is a good example of a tool being designed for a purpose which was identified as the research proceeded. A need arose to discover further evidence of the influences acting on a head of centre by establishing the social networks within which he worked. Therefore, each head of centre interviewed was asked to complete the task below.

Please list every *work related* * *contact*† you make with individuals or groups who are not either members of your staff or students/members of your institution, during the week commencing Monday 8 November, and ending Sunday 14 November (inclusive).

  * *work related* – what is work related must be your decision;
  if you feel that the contact has some work-related content please
  record it.

  † *contact* – by telephone or correspondence (both incoming and
  outgoing) as well as face to face.

We might have asked for a diary over a longer period; we might have
checked on the relative intensities of contacts; however, early attempts
by a group of volunteers to keep a more detailed diary posed them far
too many problems and we had no wish to impose even more on very
busy people who had already given so much of their time.

References

1. **Filstead, W. J.** (1970) *Qualitative Methodology*, Chicago, p. 8.
2. **Glaser, B. G. and Strauss, A. L.** (1967) *The Discovery of Grounded Theory*,
   Chicago, p. 45.
3. **Pilsworth, M. and Ruddock, R.** (1975) 'Some criticisms of survey research methods
   in adult education', *Convergence*, **8**, No. 2, p. 41.

Chapter 3

Some basic concepts in adult education

Making a working philosophy

Every educator wants to be able to explain and justify his work to himself, to those whose opinion he values (employers, clients and professional colleagues) and, since he spends public money, to society at large. To do this he must find some answers to the question: 'What should I be doing, and for whom?' The answers will provide the basis for a working philosophy which will define for him his role and his proper functions as an adult educator and which, though it may well not be completely organised and explicit, will certainly be implicit in the choices that he makes and the decisions that he takes.

This building of a working philosophy is something which each adult educator has to do for himself. But it is not, of course, done in isolation. He inherits a body of experience and tradition which is transmitted to him in various ways, sometimes formally through conferences and training courses, more frequently informally through his contacts with colleagues and with students. From all this he absorbs those ideas which seem most relevant to his job and most apt to his temperament and attitudes; these are the elements out of which a working philosophy will be formed. If he is an adult educator working in Britain in the late twentieth century he will have an unusually rich and varied body of experience and tradition upon which to draw, and this he will find already roughly codified into basic sets of ideas. These are answers, or possible answers, to the question, What? and for whom? Some will be related more directly to the first half of the question and some to the second, but these are obviously so interdependent that we can regard them all as different concepts of the function of adult education. The resonance and the significance of these different concepts of function change from time to time and from place to place: now one seems relevant and important, now another. There are five which seemed to our interviewees to be the key concepts, the basic sets of ideas, for adult educators in Britain in the 1970s: each of them offers a challenge which every adult educator must meet. We have labelled them for ease of reference, though arbitrarily:

1. *Teaching;*
2. *Recreation;*
3. *Participation;*
4. *Compensation;*
5. *Community;*

In what follows we try to show how they are related to one another and what are their salient characteristics. The order in which they are presented is that which seems to us to bring out most clearly their interrelations and the logical links between them, and does not imply any judgment about their relative importance.

Five basic concepts

1. To the question, 'What should I be doing?' the *Teaching* or *Didactic* concept gives an apparently simple answer: if the adult educator is an educator then he must be one who teaches or who enables and helps others to teach. It is the presence of teaching not of learning (it is claimed) that is the defining characteristic of education, for teaching is specific to educational situations but learning is not. We can learn in all the circumstances of life and we learn more, and more important things, outside of educational situations than we do inside them. So we certainly cannot say that where there is learning there must have been education. But we can say that where there is education there must be teaching – which has, of course, the intention of producing learning.

The *Teaching* concept postulates the establishment of a particular kind of interpersonal relationship, which may be formal or quite informal, in which one person (who accepts the role of teacher, tutor, etc.) attempts to help others (who accept the role of learner, student, etc.) to learn and attempts also to guide their learning towards desirable ends. For it is plain that learning is not necessarily good or desirable in itself: we can learn incompetencies, bad habits and error as easily as (more easily than?) skills, good habits and truth. An adult is a free agent and therefore enters into such a relationship voluntarily and on a basis of equality, unlike the child or the adolescent who may be subject to coercion or to strong suasion. So the relationship between teacher and adult student, though it remains an educational one, differs in some respects from that between teacher and child or adolescent; it implies, for example, negotiation between teacher and student about what are desirable ends and how they shall be pursued. Different organisational and institutional patterns may also be implied, as well as different teaching methods.

Because education which is undertaken voluntarily must normally be undertaken when the adult student has time at his own disposal, i.e. in his leisure, adult education is often described as education *for* leisure. From the point of view of the *Teaching* concept this is false: adult education is 'for' whatever educators and students hold to be the ends of education generally or of their course in particular.

2. The *Recreation* concept is grounded in the notion which the *Teaching* concept rejects: that adult education is indeed education *for*

leisure. But it asserts the growing importance of leisure in modern society. Recreation in leisure can provide (it is claimed) a means of compensating for the boredom and frustration engendered by repetitive and uncreative work and of reducing the loneliness which is so characteristic a product of urban and suburban living conditions. So what is from the *Teaching* or *Didactic* point of view a by-product of adult education – the recreational and social satisfactions which it gives – becomes a main objective. Leisure activities are thus valued in and for themselves irrespective of the amount or the quality of the learning that may result from them; what matters more is enjoyment of the leisure activity and social contacts themselves. From this point of view classes and courses are seen as less appropriate forms of organisation than clubs and societies and social activities, and the role of the adult educator tends to shift somewhat towards that of the social facilitator and recreation manager.

[The word 'recreation' is very often used in a much wider sense to describe any or all forms of adult education. We have tried to give it a narrower and more precise connotation, for when a word is taken to mean so much it may end up meaning very little. The argument for this wider usage runs as follows: all adult education is undertaken voluntarily and in leisure; we do voluntarily only what we enjoy doing; adult education is therefore enjoyment in leisure; enjoyment in leisure is recreation; therefore all adult education is recreation. The logic may seem dubious, but the argument is tacitly accepted by a very large number of those who form opinion and make policy in the world of education. Unfortunately it has been strengthened by what may have been initially two accidents of nomenclature. First: Section 41b of the Education Act 1944 which is usually taken to be the section governing adult education (although that was not necessarily its intention) does not use the word 'education' at all, but speaks instead of 'leisure-time occupation' and 'recreative activities'. Second: the Local Education Authorities, seeking a less cumbrous term than 'Other Further Education' to distinguish non-vocational and non-examined courses from the rest of Further Education, have come not unnaturally to use 'recreational' or 'recreative' in this sense. So the view that all adult education is recreation has become firmly embedded in the language of educational administration and is even seen as having statutory force. This has not only made it difficult to use the word in our narrower sense, it has also made it easy for those who wish to do so to denigrate adult education as 'mere' recreation.]

3. The *Participation* concept shares many of the contentions upon which the *Recreation* concept is grounded, and these need not be repeated. But it expresses them in a stronger and more active form, and it adds to them the conviction that since man is a social animal effective learning is more likely to result from co-operation with others for shared purposes than from direct *Teaching*. So social and recreational

activities are valued not only for themselves but also for what from the *Recreation* point of view is a by-product – for the opportunities of joint enterprise and management and of self-government that they provide, even though these may often be upon a small scale. These opportunities may be found in plenty in the organisation itself provided that its structure and its general atmosphere are democratic: in the running of classes, clubs and societies, in the organisation of social activities and functions, and in the management of the institution itself. But they may also be found – and should it is claimed be actively sought – outside the institution in opportunities of participation in the work of local groups and organisations of many different kinds. The creation of such opportunities for social interaction and for participation in common enterprises, both inside the institution and outside in the community which it serves becomes an end in itself, and the role of the adult educator shifts somewhat towards that of the *animateur*.

4. The simplest answer to the 'for whom?' part of the question, and perhaps the answer most frequently given or taken for granted, is: 'For all who wish to take part'. This is an expression of a concept of open entry, of a non-selective principle of recruitment. It is grounded in the general conviction that in a civilised society every adult should have access to teaching or recreation or participation, and in the specific contention that in a democratic society every citizen should have a right to use an educational service which is made possible by the deployment of public funds.

The *Compenstion* concept challenges this directly and claims that this allegedly non-selective open-entry system is in practice highly selective and by no means open. The argument is based on two main contentions. First: the content of an institution's programme and the way in which this is presented and advertised have themselves (it is claimed) an obvious selective effect; they recruit only those who comprehend and are already well disposed towards what is being offered. Second: it is those who have had more than the average amount of education and who have more than the average amount of social confidence who find it easy to join adult education institutions and who tend to become their most active and influential members; they are tacitly and probably unconsciously selected by the institution. To counter these tendencies a policy of positive discrimination is proposed. Since resources are limited they should be channelled away from those who have most and towards those who have least, and both the content of programmes and methods of recruitment should be directed towards meeting the needs of the dispossessed and the disadvantaged. So adult education is seen primarily as an agency of educational and social compensation and restitution.

When it is linked with the *Teaching* concept *Compensation* is likely to be directed towards the educationally underprivileged (illiterates, innumerates, the minimally educated, etc.); adult education will be seen as having a remedial role within the educational system as a whole with the duty of trying to correct and compensate for the failures and inequities of earlier stages of public education. When it is linked with the *Recreation* concept *Compensation* is likely to be directed towards the biologically and economically underprivileged (the physically and mentally handicapped, the old, the poor, etc.); adult education will be seen as having a generally ameliorative function rather than a specifically educational one: it becomes an expression of *caritas*, a means of caring. When it is linked with the *Participation* concept *Compensation* is likely to be directed towards getting people actively engaged in compensatory and caring and reforming groups and ventures; adult education is seen as having a part to play in community development and social reform.

5. The answer given to the question 'What should I be doing and for whom?' may be based upon an assumption of discontinuity or of continuity between the different parts of the educational system. The first produces the contention that adult education is a separable sector of education with purposes, methods of work and modes of recruitment which are quite clearly different from those of other sectors; it should therefore develop its own patterns of organisation and its own institutions.

The continuity assumption challenges this view and emphasises the unity rather than the diversity which (it is claimed) underlies apparently different aspects or phases of education. Thus the continuity of (post-school) vocational and non-vocational education is frequently asserted, and this leads to the linking of the two in such institutions as Colleges of Further Education. Since this post-school vocational education is very largely addressed to the 16–19 age group the linking of these can lead to an assertion of continuity between adult and adolescent education, though it need not do so. Indeed an assumption of continuity between the education of youths and adults very often goes along with an assumption of discontinuity between vocational and non-vocational education. This leads to the linking of adult education with youth service, i.e. with non-vocational youth groups which have, on the whole, a lower age range than that found in Colleges of Further Education.

But the most thorough-going expression of continuity is the *Community* concept as embodied in such institutions as Community Schools and Colleges. Their claim is that education is a continuous and lifelong process, and that it should not be artificially divided into separate sectors or stages. Instead it should be conceived as a totality and administered through institutions which provide for the whole range of educational needs from childhood through adolescence to adulthood and old age. Adult education therefore ceases to exist as a separate entity with separate institutions; it is replaced by community education which is addressed to all age groups and all sectors in the population. Many of these institutions are relatively young and, of course, some discontinuities remain in them. The vocational/non-vocational division remains, for vocational education addressed to adolescents and adults tends to be excluded from community institutions. Nor is the school/post-school discontinuity always entirely removed. Thus when a Community School or College speaks of 'community education' it sometimes means its total educational provision including that for the school children in the population, but it sometimes means its provision for other than school children, i.e. for youths and adults. Nevertheless, these institutions represent the most determined attempt that has been made to break down the barriers between one phase of education and another.

From our point of view the most important aspect of the *Community* concept is its attempt to make open entry an active instead of a passive principle by reaching out to and co-operating with the widest possible variety of groups and organisations in the catchment population – including those identified by the *Compensation* concept but ranging far wider. Thus it shifts the centre of gravity of decision making and programme planning out of the educational institution and into the population which it serves. So (it is claimed) policy will be made and programmes determined by the wants and needs of the community rather than by the convictions and judgments of the community educator. (The much used phrase 'the needs of the community' begs many questions, of course, but the general tenor of the argument is clear.)

The *Community* concept can, like the *Compensation* concept, work in harness with any of the others. But it tends to fit most happily alongside the *Recreation* and the *Participation* concepts, for these offer the widest and the most eclectic range of contacts with the catchment population.

[The word 'community', like 'recreation', has been given such a wide connotation that it becomes difficult to use it with any precision at all. We have restricted our use of it to the narrower connotation that it has in, for example, 'Community College' or 'Community School', where it implies a view of education as a totality continuing throughout childhood, adolescence and adulthood involving a commitment to participation in all aspects of the life of the catchment population. But we have noted six other ways in which such a term as 'community education' is used:
- the education of adolescents jointly with adults;
- education addressed to the 'community' meaning by this the local population generally;
- education addressed to those sectors of the population not usually reached by conventional adult education;
- education addressed to the deprived and disadvantaged;
- education directed towards the creation of a sense of community;
- education directed towards local action and community development.

No doubt there are others; indeed the word 'community' seems at times to be in danger of becoming no more than a slogan.]

Philosophies and institutions

These, then, are some of the concepts with which the contemporary adult educator will build his working philosophy. They are not, of course, mutually exclusive and accepting one does not mean rejecting the rest. They co-exist, interact and modify one another, and most adult educators are likely to find most of them valid and usable, one in one context and one in another. Where adult educators will differ, and differ markedly, will be in the different degrees of emphasis or priority that they give to these ideas and in the way in which they deal with the conflicts and tensions between them. Conflict and tension is inescapable, but though their effects can be inhibitory they can also be creative. With experience they will be accommodated within a reasonably coherent and consistent working philosophy. How this is done will depend upon the interplay between, on the one hand, the adult educator's own values and attitudes and, on the other, the pressures exerted by the demands of employers, the expectations of students, the opinions of colleagues and the nature of the institution in which he works.

No doubt there are connections, too, between these different concepts and different institutional patterns, and some of the implications of these will be referred to later. In institutions as in philosophies different concepts will co-exist, and the differences between institutions, like those between philosophies, are likely to be matters of priority and emphasis. Nevertheless some types of institution can obviously accommodate some concepts of function more easily than others. The traffic between idea and institution can, of course, flow in both directions: sometimes the idea has clearly generated the institution; sometimes the institution has been formed in accordance with considerations which have little to do with adult education but then adopts or generates ideas about adult education to fit itself. This two-way traffic is normal and necessary, for without it new ideas would be less likely to be developed.

But though these connections between idea and institution clearly exist and though they usually produce a reasonable consonance between the two, they are neither simple nor invariable. Indeed the remarkable thing is the wide range of variance which exists between institutions which are apparently of the same type and which seem to be operating in similar circumstances. This must in part be accounted for by the traditional freedom which the adult educator in this country has to develop his own philosophy and to build the institution for which he is responsible in the light of that philosophy. It was certainly plain from our many conversations with professional adult educators up and down the country that most of them were conscious of that freedom and valued the creative dimension which it added to their role.

Chapter 4

A typology of institutions

These are at least seven ways in which adult education institutions could be described and classified. Differences between them could be measured along any of the following dimensions:

- Formal linkages (with Colleges of Further Education, Schools, Youth Service, Leisure Services – or with none of these);
- Staffing (full-, part- and spare-time; status);
- Environment (demographic; economic; educational);
- Size (number of courses, of students, of student hours);
- Teaching accommodation (own, hired, borrowed and shared premises);
- Management (degree of autonomy; professional and lay participation);
- Philosophy (dominant concept of purpose).

If we were dealing with factories instead of adult education institutions we should assume that each of these seven variables influenced in some way the product of the factory, and we should try to isolate and measure the influence of each. But it did not require much experimenting to persuade us that such procedures, however logical and scientific they may seem, were quite inappropriate to the institutions and problems with which we were trying to deal. There are two main and, it seemed to us, insuperable difficulties.

The first is that whereas the product of a factory is clearly identifiable and measurable the product of an adult education institution is not. Its ultimate product is presumably some change in its students, some increment, if the institution is working effectively, of skill, knowledge, sensibility and understanding. But such changes are often neither immediate (they may at first be only latent) nor observable (except to close associates) nor measurable (without a quite unacceptable apparatus of regular observation and testing). If a team of participant observers were to work in one institution for several years they could probably establish sufficiently close relations with a sufficient number of students to get within sight of what we have called the ultimate product of the institution. But such an exercise was clearly beyond our resources. So we fell back upon what may be called the proximate product of an adult education institution – its programme, regarded as a statement of intention and, to some degree, of performance. (The limitations of programmes as evidence, and the ways in which they may nevertheless be used, are discussed in Chapter 5.)

When the first difficulty has been resolved (or evaded) by the identification and description of the proximate product, we encounter the second one. Normally one would seek to isolate the influence upon the product of any one variable by observing the effect of changes in that variable when the other six are held constant. What makes this a virtually impossible task is the enormously wide range of variance within each variable – sometimes wider than the differences between them. Thus, suppose we were trying to isolate and measure the effect of changes in (say) mode of Management. At how many institutions should we have to look to find (say) ten which differed in this respect but were the same in respect of Size, Environment, Staffing, Accommodation, Philosophy and Linkages? Certainly at many thousands, and this again was clearly an impossible task.

So we had to go to work in a different way. We shelved for a time the question of typology, read through many hundreds of statements, questionnaires and programmes, and began the slow business of visiting institutions and interviewing adult educators. From this (at this stage) unorganised profusion of evidence tentative notions began to emerge about the nature of these variables. These in turn suggested that certain kinds of new evidence were needed, and the new evidence in turn altered or sharpened the emerging notions. As this systole and diastole of data collection and concept formation proceeded ideas about the rationale of these variables and about the connections between them grew firmer, and they began to assume a rough rank order. In what follows we describe the variables as we see them, listing them roughly in order of importance, and then go on to build them into a very simple typology.

1. Formal linkages with other institutions and agencies. There may of course be no such association: adult education can be and often has been a separate and specialised service with its own separate and specialised institutions (such as the Mechanics Institutes or the Educational Settlements). But this is not now generally the case, and for a very good reason. Adult education is, as we all know, a minority pursuit; not only does it engage, at any one time, a quite small proportion of the adult population (though the proportion becomes substantial over a period of time), it also engages that minority for quite small periods of time, perhaps a couple of hours a week for twenty to thirty weeks, a year or even less. So if a separate and specialised institution – and its staff – is to be fully used it must have either an unusually substantial or an unusually responsive catchment population to draw upon. Where this is not, or is not thought to be, feasible and economically justifiable adult education has to look to other institutions and agencies to which it can attach itself. Again there is nothing new in this – witness the long-standing connection between the Workers' Educational Association and the Universities – but it is rapidly becoming the norm. There are three main modes of attachment.

(a) Adult education is given the right to use school premises without payment when they are not needed by the school: the school is the lender and adult education the borrower or, to put it in another way, the school is the host institution and adult education the lodger. The host may be willing or unwilling, and the linkage between host and lodger may be tight or loose. But lodgement of this kind clearly involves a more complex relationship than would a simple commercial transaction such as the hiring of a room.

(b) A closer relationship is established; the lodger moves into and becomes, through various stages, part of the host institution; lodgement (or parasitism as the unsympathetic might describe it) gives place to sharing (or symbiosis). Finally, adult education is seen not as a separate service but as one of the functions of the host institution which, as a result, may itself be re-defined and enlarged. The most common hosts are Colleges of Further Education and Community Schools – with Leisure Centres also beginning to claim a place.

(c) Adult education is not absorbed by but is yoked with a service which is seen as closely related to it to form a new, joint service. The usual partner is youth service, and since youth service like adult education is a scattered service with few substantial institutions of its own the two combine to form a new, specialised and separate adult-and-youth service. In theory this should be a yoking of equals: in practice either may become the dominant partner.

2. Staffing The importance of this variable is, like that of the preceding one, implicit in the basic nature and structure of adult education in this country. In this case the relevant fact is that adult education is a widely dispersed service organised, in general, in small units. It follows that the influence of the professional adult educator is correspondingly large: the presence or the absence of one professional or even half a one, as in a joint appointment, can make all the difference to the life and work of any one institution.

Different types of appointment need therefore to be clearly differentiated, and current usage clarified. One cause of confusion is that all appointments which are not full-time are customarily referred to as 'part-time'; this obscures an important distinction and to bring this out three categories are needed, not two.

(a) A person may hold a full-time post in adult education; he may be what in other spheres would be called a 'career' adult educator. We call him a full-time adult educator.

(b) He may hold a post in which he has a joint responsibility, part of his time being given to adult education and part to youth service, school-teaching or vocational Further Education. We call him a part-time adult educator.

(c) He may earn his living by full-time employment in some other field altogether (perhaps school teaching or local government) but be employed as an adult educator in his spare time (as a tutor or a head of centre). We call him a spare-time adult educator.

To some extent the distinction between these three types of appointment is a quantitative one: the authority that makes a part-time appointment gives more man-hours to adult education than the authority that makes a spare-time appointment, but fewer man-hours than the authority that makes a full-time appointment. But there may also be qualitative differences. The full-time adult educator will see himself as a professional and will think of his career in terms of adult education; he is, in every sense of the word, committed. The part-time adult educator is not so completely committed; he has two possible careers and can switch from one to the other if it seems prudent to do so. The spare-time adult educator may seem the least committed of all, and so no doubt he generally is. But he may feel another kind of commitment: he may be doing this job in his leisure because he likes doing it rather than simply for the financial reward; he may to some extent be a volunteer and this voluntary element may sometimes give his work a supererogatory zest and quality.

3. Environment Our first thought was that this would be the most important variable of all: density of population, age and employment structure, levels of wealth and of education – surely all these must have a decisive influence upon the nature and work of an adult education institution. A big population can support a big institution, the well-to-do can pay high fees, leisured people can give time to committees as well as classes and, most important of all, the people with most education are the ones who are most likely both to want more and to know where and how to get it. All this is beyond dispute. Yet two institutions in (apparently) the same environment may be very different and two institutions in (apparently) quite different environments may be very similar. It is, in fact, surprisingly difficult at times to establish a direct relationship between environmental and institutional characteristics. There are three reasons for this:

(a) It is in practice very difficult to define the catchment population for any particular institution; it may for some purposes draw only upon its immediate neighbourhood of one or two thousand people, but for others students may travel considerable distances and the catchment population may increase to tens of thousands.

(b) The institution will, consciously or unconsciously, through its policy, its programme and its contacts, select its students from the possible catchment population. It can, after all, serve only a minority of that population. But, of many possible minorities, which will it recruit and serve? Through the choices and decisions, often small in themselves, which combine to provide an answer to that question the institution defines and to some extent creates its own population and its own environment.

(c) Lastly, even when the catchment population can be defined it is very difficult to match this with available demographic, economic or educational statistics: the statistical units are usually too big, and rarely coincide with the adult educational ones.

So, after many attempts, we abandoned the idea of any close matching of environment and institution and have found four broad and ill-defined but generally understood categories adequate to our purposes. They are: large cities; middle-size and small towns; suburban and commuter areas; rural areas. For some purposes it is sufficient simply to distinguish between densely populated and sparsely populated or between urban and rural areas.

4. Size   Clearly the size of an institution is partly dependent upon the size and density of the catchment population, but not wholly so: though one may not find large institutions in small villages there are large centres in small towns and small centres in large cities. In turn, size of centre affects the level and the degree of specialisation of staffing and accommodation although, like size of population, it is a limiting factor only: specialist staff and premises are unlikely to be found in institutions below a certain size but there is no certainty that they will be found in those above it. Two questions arise:

(a) How does one measure size? The best indicator would be the number of student-hours or, failing that, the number of users or of enrolled students. But reliable and comparable estimates of student-hours or usage or even of enrolment are hard to come by, so we have had to use the number of courses offered as our main indicator of size.

(b) What is an institution? We are faced with a continuum with at one end the large city centre which may have satellite subcentres attached to it, in the middle the market-town centre with a programme of its own but also the responsibility for ten or a dozen centres in the surrounding rural area, and at the other end the scatter of twenty or thirty village centres with only an area or a regional office to report to. Both the first and the second should clearly be treated as single institutions. The third we have treated as a single institution when the general control of policy and programme seems to be centred at the area headquarters rather than in the individual centres. This always implies the presence, at area level, of a specialist adult educator who usually has some teaching as well as administrative accommodation at his disposal. But the distinction is by no means clear or easy to establish.

5. Accommodation   It is of course teaching, not administrative, accommodation that is for us the important criterion. There are three main possibilities: an institution may work in

(a) premises which are its own in the sense of being entirely at its

disposal (including premises which are hired);
(b) premises which are borrowed (dual usage);
(c) premises which are those of a host institution which has adult education as one of its functions and which adult education therefore shares;

or, of course some mixture of these. These three categories are referred to in Section 1 (Formal linkages) above, but we have thought it important to distinguish the second from the third. The term 'dual usage' applies only to the second, when two different organisations (an adult education institution and, say, a school) are using the same premises for different purposes and at different times. Strictly speaking the third category should be regarded as mono usage, not dual usage, for only one institution is involved; this should, but does not always, result in greater flexibility and less friction.

6. *Management* A main issue is the degree of autonomy of the institution, which in turn is strongly influenced by the methods of control employed by the responsible authority:
(a) Maximal control is exercised when the authority determines levels of student fees, enrolment and attendance minima, duration of courses, etc. and when grant is allocated (e.g. to tutor fees, clerical assistance, equipment) without any possibility of transfer.
(b) Minimal control is exercised when grant is given as a total sum. The institution is thus free to allocate this as it wishes and to set whatever levels of student fees, enrolment requirements, etc. it thinks desirable and (within this total expenditure) economically possible.
(c) There is an intermediate level of control in which the authority determines minimum levels of enrolment, etc. but allows these to be interpreted as applying to average levels in the institution as a whole, not separately to each course, class or activity.

When we speak of the degree of autonomy of an adult education institution we are really speaking of the degree of autonomy of the adult educator or educators who manage it: it is people, not institutions, who exercise or lose freedom. Clearly this will be affected by patterns of management as well as by financial controls, and in particular by:

the relation of the professional adult educator to lay bodies such as Student Councils;
the status of the adult educator in the hierarchy of institutions with which adult education is linked or by which it is absorbed;
the size and effectiveness of the supporting administrative and technical services at his disposal.

7. *Philosophy* We use the term in a quite simple and non-tecinical sense to mean the kind of answers that an adult educator might give to the questions: What should I as an adult educator be doing? For whom should I be doing it? The issues are discussed in Chapter 3, in which five

basic concepts are identified and described. These will obviously affect, and be affected by, institutional patterns.

The major types of adult education institution

We distinguish five major groups of institutions:

Sp.	(Specialised)
FE.	(Colleges of Further Education)
Comm.	(Community Schools and Colleges)
AY	(Adult plus Youth)
L	(Leisure)

Their overall general characteristics, in terms of the seven variables discussed above, are set out below – with two caveats:

(a) These are highly generalised descriptions of dominant tendencies. They try to identify the centre of gravity in each group, not to make a sharp delineation of boundaries, which are bound to overlap.

(b) There is a wide range of variance within each group – greater, in some cases, than the difference between groups, so that a particular institution may well seem not to fit easily into the generalised description of the group. This does not, of course, mean that the descriptions of group characteristics are invalid or that they do not fit most institutions in the group. It simply means that we must be prepared to find in each group a few, but often marked, eccentricities and exceptions.

Group Sp.   Adult education is conceived as a distinguishable and separate sector of education, needing to develop its own organisation and institutions and capable of doing so. This is a widespread (though probably diminishing) institutional type capable of operating in all kinds of habitats, but size, patterns of staffing and availability of teaching accommodation will vary in a continuum from high-density urban and suburban areas to low-density rural areas. In urban areas there will tend to be specialised adult education centres staffed by full-time adult educators (often including some full-time teachers) and with their own teaching accommodation: schools may be used as satellite centres and in these some spare-time organising staff may be employed, but policy making is clearly in the hands of full-time professionals. At the other end of the continuum, in low-density rural areas, provision will be dispersed over a number of small centres using borrowed (mainly school) accommodation and run by spare-time adult educators. These may be virtually independent, in which case policy making will have shifted completely from the full-time to the spare-time adult educator. Or there may be intermediate stages in which the independence of the spare-time adult educator is limited by the presence of a relatively small number of full-time area adult education organisers or advisers. It is in the institutions of this group (Sp.) that adult education finds its greatest degree of independence and autonomy.

Four sub-types need to be distinguished; though, again, there are no hard and fast boundaries between them:

1. Full-time staff including teachers and other specialists; own teaching accommodation; large institutions mainly in cities and suburban areas.
2. Some full-time staff (but usually only one); borrowed teaching accommodation; medium-size institutions mainly in towns.
3. Mainly spare-time staff; borrowed teaching accommodation; generally small urban institutions.
4. Almost wholly spare-time staff; borrowed teaching accommodation; generally small rural institutions.

Group FE. Adult education is conceived as part of Further Education (as, statutorily, it is) and as continuous with the Further Education of the 16–19-year-olds. It is therefore absorbed by and becomes one of the functions of Colleges of Further Education. Probably most such Colleges offer a few non-vocational courses, but we are not concerned with these. We are concerned only with those Colleges in which adult education is a recognised sector of their work making a substantial contribution to total student-hours, and which are used by the providing authority as a main agency for the promotion and organisation of adult education in the area served. These will tend to have an urban base since they must have a catchment population big enough to support their normal work, but they may also serve a suburban or rural area. Adult education appointments will tend to be technically part-time, but may often be in effect full-time. If a large area is served there may be satellite centres run either by full-time or spare-time adult educators. Since all the work of the College (including adult education) is Further Education there will usually be no separate budget; adult education has to compete for funds with the other departments of the College. On the other hand this access to general Further Education funds may protect it when authorities are having to cut their ear-marked grants to adult education. Policy decisions must ultimately rest with the principal, and in this type of institution adult education's loss of autonomy is in theory complete. But in practice this may not be so, for there is in Colleges of Further Education a strong tradition of departmental independence and enterprise both in devising courses and recruiting students. So, provided that the goodwill of the principal and the academic board be retained, the loss of autonomy may be more apparent than real.

There are probably two sub-types that can usefully be distinguished, though the boundary between them is by no means clear.

1. Full-time and part-time staff; adult education has departmental status; shared teaching accommodation; medium to large institutions.

2. Mainly part-time staff; adult education does not have departmental status; shared teaching accommodation; medium to small institutions.

Group Comm. Adult education is conceived, along with youth service, as continuous with schooling and as one of the functions of the school, which is then usually designated a Community School. Historically this is a rural concept and its natural habitat seems to be rural areas, although an urban variant is developing. It is often claimed that such a school exemplifies a commitment to continuing or permanent education serving all age-groups in the community. But in fact the commitment to post-school education may be a narrow one, for Further and Higher Education as usually defined, tend to be excluded. From the point of view of adult education this means that it is disconnected from those sectors of education with which it might seem to have a more natural affinity and connected instead with a sector of education (the school) with which, because of its age range and its compulsory nature, it might seem to have least affinity. There are financial discontinuities as well, for in these institutions (unlike those of FE.) the different aspects of their work (school, youth and adult) are separately financed. The adult educator in the Community School usually holds a part-time (joint) appointment, combining with adult education some responsibility for youth and/or school work; there are of course exceptions to this, but by and large the part-time adult educator is the characteristic figure in these institutions. As in Group FE., control of policy rests ultimately with the principal and loss of autonomy is in theory complete. Nor is it mitigated, as in FE., by such a strong tradition of departmental independence. In practice, of course, personal goodwill and tolerance can establish a reasonable delegation of power.

There are two main, and very different, sub-types of which the first is the major one:

1. Long-established: small and medium-size rural and suburban institutions; part-time staff; shared teaching accommodation.
2. More recently established: very large multi-purpose institutions but with relatively small adult education programmes; urban inner-city or re-housing areas; part-time staff; shared teaching accommodation.

Group AY Adult education is conceived, not as an aspect of the work of other educational institutions (as in FE. and Comm.) but as a specialised and dispersed sector of education which can best be developed jointly with a similar specialised and dispersed sector. This is a yoking of two (notionally) equal partners, not (as in FE. and Comm.) the absorption of one by the other. The obvious partner for adult education is youth service. Both are voluntary, both are widely dispersed and neither has the independence which would be given by the possession of a network of large and established institutions such as schools or Colleges of Further Education: it is to some extent an alliance of the dispossessed. So this new joint service will have to create its own organisation and institutions, as has Group Sp. Unlike that it will, since it has a dual function, make joint appointments of part-time adult educators and part-time youth organisers. But though it is substantially a part-time service centrally this may weaken as one moves down towards local levels, where integration may weaken and members of staff may sort themselves out, according to their interest, experience and training, into virtually full-time adult educators or youth leaders. Teaching accommodation will be mainly borrowed, though there may be some sharing of youth service premises. Satellite centres may be run by spare-time staff.

1. Urban areas; part-time with some (effectively) full-time staff; borrowed, with some shared, premises; medium-size institutions.
2. Smaller urban institutions; spare-time with some part-time staff; borrowed with some shared premises.

Group L   Adult education is conceived as an aspect of entertainment or recreation rather than education and thus comes within the purview of a Recreation and Leisure Services Committee or the like. This is a recent development and its institutional implications have still to be worked out. It might lead simply to the attachment of adult education to a dispersed network of leisure services, in which case it would be a new sub-group in AY. Or it might lead (as has indeed happened in a few places) to the assimilation of adult education as one of the functions of the new institutions called Leisure Centres. Neither of these developments has gone far enough for us to feel able to offer any comments about them, but they are of potential importance.

Chapter 5

Curriculum analysis:
a subject classification

In discussing the performance of different types of adult education institution one set of questions which obviously has to be asked concerns their programmes: what do they teach? what proportion of their resources is given to this group of subjects or to that? and so on. These are questions which it is particularly important to ask about institutions of adult education since they are free of many of the external pressures operating upon, for example, Further Education establishments and schools which have to meet the demands of external examinations and career qualifications, or have to teach certain subjects because a national consensus of opinion defines them as basic subjects or because Universities regard them as entrance requirements. Adult education institutions are free of such pressures; the range of choices open to them seems virtually limitless, or is limited only by their ability to recruit interested students. So we do need to know what is taught and how institutions differ from one another in what they teach.

The most immediate source of evidence about what is taught was the large collection of published programmes which we were building up. Programmes have certain obvious shortcomings as evidence of provision: brief titles of courses yield very little information about them; not all courses that are announced in a programme take place, and not all courses that take place are announced in the programme. But we had to use this evidence as best we could in spite of its limitations, and to hope that the limitations would be sufficiently constant over the whole field to enable us to make comparisons between different groups of institutions within it. Moreover, the evidence of interviews suggested that programmes do in general provide a more complete picture of provision than is commonly maintained and that they are in a real sense what we have called the 'proximate product' of adult education institutions.

We had to find a system of subject classification that was conceptually simple (for short titles provide no basis for fine discriminations) and easy to use. There is always a strong case for using an already existing system of classification, so we looked hard at the systems used by the (then) Ministry of Education in *Statistics of Education* (up to 1958) and by the National Institute of Adult Education in *Adequacy of Provision* (1970). In the end we rejected them both as beyond the limitations both of our time and of the material itself. So we started to look at the problem of subject classification again from the beginning.

There are at least three possible bases for a classification of courses:
(a) the educational objective of the course (e.g. the development of aesthetic physical or intellectual skills);
(b) the objective of the course as it is perceived by the putative student (e.g. career advancement, household competence, leisure pastime);
(c) the sector of the population to which the course is addressed (e.g. women, fishermen, the well-educated, immigrants).

The logical thing to do would be to choose one of these as a basis for classification and stick to it; to mix them would seem to invite confusion. Yet this is what in the end we decided to do, our main reason being the conviction that it is in terms of a mixture of these categories that adult educators actually think and work and plan their programmes. They are concerned with (a) for this is what they have in mind when they worry about a 'balanced' programme; they are concerned with (b) for there are established areas of student interest which they ignore at their peril; and they are concerned with (c) for they want to recruit from all the major sectors of their local population and perhaps particularly from the less well-endowed sectors. We concluded that the main categories that the adult educator might have at the back of his mind when planning his programme were these:

Crafts and Arts;
Physical Activities and Games;
Intellectual or Cognitive Studies;
Vocational and Examination-Directed Courses;
Courses for the Disadvantaged.

After some experiment we decided to omit the category concerning vocational and examination courses, not because they are unimportant (indeed they are a growing part of many programmes) but because they are particularly subject to administrative restrictions which may differ widely from place to place and so produce a wildly fluctuating picture. (Thus, one authority may encourage such courses, another may exclude them from adult education provision, another may approve RSA courses but may reserve all O-level teaching to other institutions, and so on.) Experiment also suggested that Categories 1, 2 and 3 could usefully be subdivided according to the student's probable view of the objective of the course, and indeed they were often so subdivided in the mind of the programme planner. These revisions produced a classification with four main categories and six sub-categories, as follows:
1. Craft and Aesthetic Skills
    1.1 Courses related mainly to personal care and the household economy
    1.2 Courses related mainly to leisure time enjoyment
2. Physical Skills
    2.1 Courses related mainly to the maintenance of health and fitness

    2.2 Courses related mainly to leisure time enjoyment
3. Intellectual and Cognitive Skills
    3.1 Language Courses
    3.2 Other Courses
4. Courses addressed to Disadvantaged Groups.

Category 4 presents a special problem since it is at this point that the classification shifts from a subject to a student basis, so that any course in 4 could just as logically be classified in 1, 2 and 3 according to its subject. So we set ourselves the rule that Category 4 should have precedence over the others and that any course that could be assigned there should be so assigned. Thus, if a course is addressed to immigrants or to the old it goes into Category 4 no matter what its subject matter may be.

    Clearly these categories are not wholly exclusive; there is often only a vague borderline between them, and when the evidence is only a title in a programme there may well be doubt about where it should be assigned. When in doubt we have compromised and divided courses between the two categories in dispute. But most can be placed with reasonable certainty. And our judgments or misjudgments are likely to have been reasonably consistent throughout and so should not invalidate broad comparisons between different groups of institutions. Examples of the way in which subjects have been allocated are given in Appendix C.

The current curriculum of adult education

To know what is taught in adult education is at least as important as to know how it is organised. Yet the appropriate questions seem to be rarely asked, and answers to them seem peculiarly hard to come by. For a start, no national statistics showing subject distribution in adult education have been collected for twenty years. Such information was published in *Statistics of Education* up to 1958, in which year the subject analysis was discontinued – after consultation with, and with the agreement of, the Local Education Authorities who, apparently, did not think that the necessary local information was worth the trouble of collecting. Failing national statistics there are two major special enquiries to turn to: the National Institute of Adult Education's *Adequacy of Provision* (1970) and the statistical appendices to the Russell Report, *Adult Education: a Plan for Development* (1973). In spite of the three-year gap between publication dates both are based upon data gathered in the session 1968–69, so both are now somewhat dated. Moreover, Russell unfortunately follows the example of published DES statistics, which have not detailed the curriculum since 1958, although of course it brings together much valuable and otherwise unobtainable information upon such matters as staffing and finance. So the report of the National Institute of Adult Education is our only recent source of information on subject distribution. Valuable though this is, it should be remembered that it is not and was not intended to be a national survey of provision. The sample upon which it was based is small; seven authorities and 1,139 students (in Local Education Authority classes) only. Moreover, these seven authorities were chosen not as a representative sample of adult education provision but as a representative sample of the 'socio-occupational composition' of the population of England and Wales. So these figures can hardly be regarded as giving a usable picture of national subject distribution and have been much criticised on this count unfairly, for this was not the main intention of an extremely valuable survey.

Lacking national statistics, we hoped that Local Education Authorities themselves might have continued to collect data on subject distribution. So we asked if we might see any record of provision listed under subjects or subject groups which they had readily available, making it plain that we did not want to put them to the trouble of searching files or making special enquiries. But most authorities did not, it appeared, have such information readily available nor do they collect it as a matter of course; presumably they ceased to do so when the DES no longer requested it. We were therefore forced to consider the possibility of a do-it-yourself job. We could only do what was within the powers of a very small research team which for half of its time consisted of a man and a half and for the other half of three-quarters of a man. So we could not undertake any special enquiry; all we could do was to work from our collection of published programmes. On the basis of this, and with a not wholly impracticable widening of the net, it looked as though we might be able to give an appropriate picture of the curriculum of adult education in England and Wales as a whole.

Our enquiry concentrates upon 131 institutions, most of which were visited; these were drawn from twenty-six Local Education Authorities and from all the nine Standard Regions of England and Wales. To the programmes of these institutions we added, where the sample seemed small, those of institutions of a similar type with the same Local Education Authority; in this way we increased the number of programmes used without significantly changing the overall pattern of distribution either between authorities or between types of institution. This gave us a total of 22,761 courses, and this we refer to as the Survey group. As a check on this we looked at another batch of programmes drawn from ten authorities not included in the twenty-six of the Survey group but similarly dispersed geographically. This gave us a total of 11,607 courses, and this we refer to as the Crosscheck group.

Table 5.1 shows the distribution of subjects in these two groups, expressed as percentages of the total number of courses. The subject grouping used is that described above. Column 1 shows the subject distribution for the Survey group and column 2 the distribution for the Crosscheck group; column 3 shows the difference between the two.

Table 5.1   Subject distribution (percentage of total). Survey and Crosscheck

	Survey group (22,761 courses)	Crosscheck group (11,607 courses)	Survey cf. Crosscheck
1. Craft and Aesthetic Skills			
1.1	33·6	34·4	—0·8
1.2	19·5	20·1	—0·6
Total 1	53·1	54·5	—1·2
2. Physical Skills			
2.1	9·3	9·4	—0·1
2.2	14·8	13·7	+1·1
Total 2	24·1	23·1	+1·0
3. Cognitive and Intellectual Skills			
3.1	10·9	11·7	—0·8
3.2	5·8	6·2	—0·4
Total 3	16·7	17·9	—1·2
4. Courses for Disadvantaged Groups			
Total 4	6·1	4·6	+1·5

The congruence of columns 1 and 2 suggests that our survey sample is not unrepresentative of provision in England and Wales as a whole. The divergencies of the Survey from the Crosscheck group (column 3) suggest that we may have been steered towards institutions and authorities in which Subject groups 1 and 3 tend to be under-represented and Subject groups 2 and, more important, 4 tend to be over-represented. But the differences, except for this last one, are not great.

If the two groups (Survey and Crosscheck) are added together they give us 34,368 courses drawn from the provision of thirty-six Local Education Authorities (seventeen counties, twelve metropolitan districts, five London and two Welsh authorities).

No systematic method of sampling was used in the selection either of institutions or authorities; they were chosen with three main considerations in mind, (*a*) availability of information and programmes, (*b*) scatter over the various institutional types, and (*c*) geographical and demographic scatter. Because we tended to concentrate upon institutions and authorities which were able to offer information and co-operation without much difficulty the Survey is likely to present a somewhat over-favourable picture of the present state of adult education, since those institutions and authorities which most readily offer help are likely to be those in which adult education is relatively well supported and well developed. On the other hand the combined group of 34,368 courses is so large, representing as it does about one-third of the authorities and perhaps one-quarter of all the LEA provided adult education courses in England and Wales, that we thought that it might be presented as giving a reasonably fair (though possibly slightly flattering) picture of the national curriculum of adult education. Table 5.2, column 1, shows the subject distribution for LEA provision nationally, and column 2 adds the Responsible Body figures (adjusted to fit the size of the Local Education Authority sample) to these to provide as complete a picture as possible of the national curriculum. At this stage of the calculations so many guesses and adjustments have had to be made that it would be foolish to claim the degree of accuracy which is implied by a decimal point. So the results are given to the nearest whole number.

Table 5.2   Subject distribution (percentage of total). National

Subject	National provision: LEA (34,368 courses)	National provision: LEA plus RB (37,428 courses)
1.1	34	30
1.2	19	18
Total 1	53	48
2.1	10	9
2.2	14	13
Total 2	24	22
3.1	12	11
3.2	6	14
Total 3	18	25
Total 4	5	5

Is this a credible picture of the way in which the people of England and Wales spend that tiny part of their leisure which they give to publicly provided adult education? If it is, it provokes many questions: How does the curriculum come to be the way it is? By what consensus and what means are its general outlines and proportions maintained with such consistency in many different places and circumstances? Is it an expression of a native cultural tradition? Is it a good way of spending the very small amount of public money given to adult education? Is it a reasonably well-balanced programme – *mens sana in corpore sano*? Or is it irrelevant to the problems which we face, as individuals or as a society? We are bound to ask such questions but would be wise not to stay for an answer, for we are not likely to get one. Such answers as can be given each of us must give for himself in the light not of research but of his own beliefs about human history and human nature.

Chapter 6

Patterns of programme

We analysed the programmes of 131 institutions, 105 of which we also visited. They were divided as follows:

Group Sp. 1 – 21; Sp. 2 – 12; Sp. 3 – 11; Sp. 4 – 14

Group FE. 1 – 17; FE. 2 – 12

Group Comm. 1 – 21; Comm. 2 – 4

Group AY 1 – 7; AY 2 – 10

We also included two institutions in Group L, but the number of such institutions is so small and they are so new that we could not venture any opinions about them and have excluded them from the tables throughout. The number of institutions in Group Comm. 2 is also very small, and they too tend to be new and highly idiosyncratic. But they are of such interest and importance that we thought it worthwhile to retain them in the tables, even though figures and comments can only be tentative and should be regarded and treated with great caution.

The figures in Table 6.1 and in the corresponding table (7.1), in Chapter 7, are arrived at in the following fashion. The number of courses in each subject group was calculated as a percentage of total provision, and these percentage scores for all the 131 institutions were then arranged in rank order. The median of these scores was then given the value of 0, around which we then had a range of possible scores from +65 to —65. These were averaged to provide a score for each group of institutions. These average scores are given to the nearest whole number only so as to avoid the misleading impression of accuracy that a decimal point or two can give.

Table 6.1   Subject groups: Rank order (131 institutions)

Type of Institution		(1) Group 1.1	(2) Group 1.2	(3) Group 2.1	(4) Group 2.2	(5) Group 3.1	(6) Group 3.2	(7) Group 4.0
Sp.	1	—21	+ 9	—15	— 4	+23	+17	+17
	2	+ 3	+ 8	—16	— 9	+15	+ 8	— 6
	3	+ 9	— 2	+ 1	— 6	+13	— 1	—17
	4	+18	+ 5	+19	+11	—30	—19	—31
FE.	1	+11	—22	+16	—15	+ 5	± 0	+12
	2	+ 7	+ 5	+ 7	— 6	— 7	— 3	+10
Comm.	1	— 5	+11	+17	— 1	— 4	+14	—14
	2	—24	—33	—27	+ 9	—31	— 7	+28
AY	1	+13	—21	—24	+27	— 1	—26	+24
	2	+17	—50	+17	+51	—50	—46	+12

This table is presented in visual form in the following figures 6.1 to 6.10

Fig. 6.1 *Sp.1*

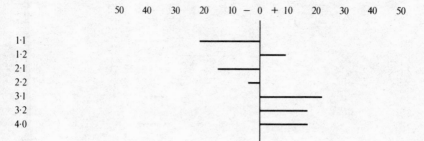

Fig. 6.2 *Sp.2*

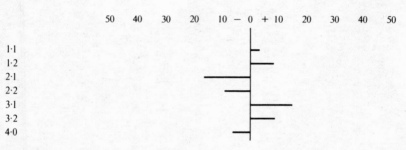

Fig. 6.3 *Sp.3*

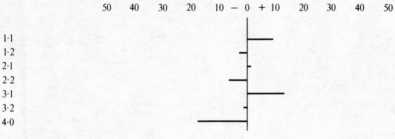

Fig. 6.4 *Sp.4*

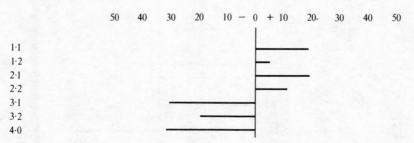

Fig. 6.5 *FE.1*

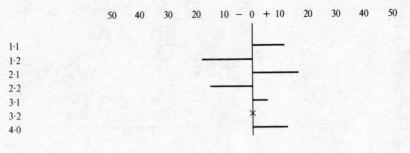

Fig. 6.6 *FE.2*

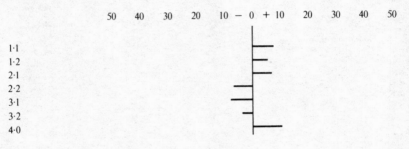

Fig. 6.7 *Comm.1*

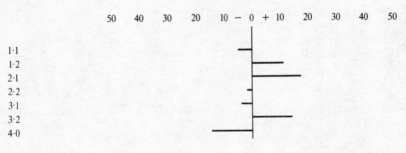

Fig. 6.8 *Comm.2*

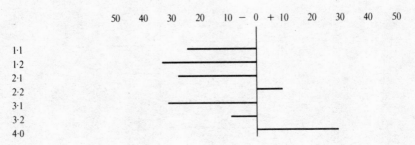

Fig. 6.9 *AY 1*

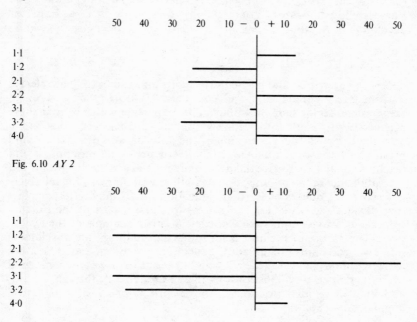

Fig. 6.10 *AY 2*

Programme patterns and institutional types

Differences between institutional types, though real, are not as clear-cut in terms of subject distribution as they are in other respects for all institutions tend (as we shall see later) to share a common core curriculum. The most obvious contrasts are the following:

Groups 1.1 and 1.2

The domestically based arts and crafts (1.1) (by far the largest subject group taking up on average one-third of all adult education provision) is fairly evenly distributed between all types of institution. Here is a public which is large and long-established and which few institutions can, it seems, ignore. Only the Specialised Institutions with their own premises (Sp. 1) and the urban Community Schools (Comm. 2) tend to displace it from its primacy. In contrast, the leisure based arts and crafts (1.2) are very much more the business of the larger Specialised Institutions (Sp. 1 and Sp. 2) and of the mainly rural Community Schools (Comm. 1) – though not, it seems, of the urban Community Schools (Comm. 2) or of the Adult and Youth organisations (AY 1 and AY 2) – or indeed of the Colleges of Further Education (particularly FE. 1), which seems a little surprising. Perhaps these are examples of the tacit influence of the host institution or of the linked organisation. If these subjects are not well developed in the normal work of Colleges of Further Education or Youth Clubs they may lack a base for development in adult education.

Groups 2.1 and 2.2

Physical activities, and particularly sports and games (2.2) are clearly a strong interest of the Adult and Youth organisations (AY 1 and AY 2); are we again seeing here the influence of the partner with which, in these organisations, adult education is joined? If such activities are a dominant part of the Youth side of the joint organisation, this – and presumably the consequent availability of premises, equipment and teachers – may help to give them a prominent place in the programme of the Adult side of the organisation as well. In a similar way the relatively low score of Colleges of Further Education on 2.2 may reflect the fact that physical activities are not normally a major part of the Further Education provision of such Colleges: another example of the way in which the nature of the host institution can (no doubt unconsciously) influence the nature of its adult education provision. Lastly, neither category of physical activities (2.1 or 2.2) seems to be a main concern of the larger Specialised Institutions (Sp. 1 and Sp. 2), though keep-fit activities (2.1) are prominent in the programmes of their rural counterparts (Sp. 4).

Groups 3.1 and 3.2

On the whole the Specialised Institutions seem to be the place for the cognitive and intellectual studies, with the exception of the rural group (Sp. 4) where catchment populations may be too small to permit the easy establishment of courses in subjects of minority interest. In this field the also mainly rural Community Schools and Colleges (Comm. 1) seem to be more successful. What is surprising is that the Colleges of Further Education do not show as well as the Specialised Institutions, particularly in language teaching (3.1) where one would have thought that they were as well endowed in staffing, in equipment and in range of experience. Our figures here may be misleading. It may well be that Colleges of Further Education provide so many language courses in their normal FE. programme and that so many of these are open to and used by adult students (a welcome example of the blurring of boundaries between vocational and non-vocational education) that it is not necessary for them to put on so large a programme of non-vocational courses specifically addressed to adults. So their work in this field is probably under-represented by the figures in the 3.1 column. At the other end of the scale, the cognitive and intellectual studies seem not to be a major concern of the urban Community Schools (Comm. 2) or of the spare-time staffed Adult and Youth organisations (AY 2).

Group 4.0

This group is commented on elsewhere, since it is a student rather than a subject group, and one of the indicators of innovative capacity.

Programmes and philosophies

There are not necessarily any direct connections to be established between different patterns of subject distribution and the different concepts of the function of adult education which have been described in Chapter 3, for in a very real sense almost any subject can be directed towards any of the purposes there discussed. Whether a course serves primarily *didactic* or *recreational* or *compensatory* or *participatory* or *community* ends depends less upon its subject than upon the way its content is selected and planned, the way it is conducted, the way it is organised and the way its students are recruited. So institutions which embody different concepts of the function of adult education may have programmes which are not markedly dissimilar in subject distribution, and apparently similar programmes may serve different purposes.

All that can be said is that although almost any subject can be used to serve almost any purpose, some subjects conform more readily to some purposes than to others. Thus it is in practice somewhat easier to use sports and games (2.2) for recreational and non-didactic purposes than it is to so use the cognitive and intellectual studies – though it is of course perfectly possible to do either. So the high proportion of Group 3.1 and 3.2 courses in the programmes of the larger Specialised Institutions (Sp. 1 and Sp. 2) is some evidence – though not, on its own, very convincing evidence – that these institutions tend to see adult education as a *teaching* activity. Other evidence reinforces this view. In interviews, heads of centre in a specialised service placed far greater emphasis on teacher training and supervision than any other category of practitioner, though the large Colleges of Further Education (FE. 1) and the Adult and Youth Service (AY 1) also identified many developments in this area. Additionally only Sp. 1 and to a much lesser extent FE. 1 have substantial numbers of graded courses: further evidence of concern for academic standards. The high proportion of leisure based physical activities (2.2) in the programmes of the Adult and Youth organisations (AY 1 and AY 2) and, to a lesser extent, in those of the urban Community Schools (Comm. 2) and the rural Specialised Institutions (Sp. 4), suggests that these institutions may tend to see adult education as recreation. But again the evidence is not, on its own, very convincing. There can, of course, be no doubt that the distribution of Group 4.0 provides clear evidence that the urban Community Schools (Comm. 2), the Adult and Youth organisations (AY 1 and AY 2), the large Specialised Institutions (Sp. 1) and, to a lesser extent, the Colleges of Further Education (FE. 1 and FE. 2) all see adult education as having an important compensatory function, but this is discussed more fully in the following chapter.

The core curriculum

Rank ordering, as used in Table 6.1, is useful as a means of comparing the performance of particular institutions or groups of institutions but it does not relate patterns of programme to any norm or reference group. This is done in Table 6.2. Column 1 is derived from Table 5.1 and shows percentage distribution of subjects in the Survey group as a whole. Column 2 shows the range and the average amount of deviation from this. Finally, column 3 expresses the average deviation shown in column 2 as a percentage of column 1, for clearly a deviation of (say) 3 per cent would be a small one in relation to a subject group which takes up 30 per cent of total provision but a large one in relation to a subject group which takes up only 6 per cent of total provision.

Table 6.2   Subject groups: Percentage deviation from norm

Subject group	(1) Percentage of total provision (from Table 5.1)	(2) Range and average deviation	(3) Average deviation as percentage of provision [(2) as percentage of (1)]
1.1	33·6	29·1 to 38·6 − ±4·7	±14·0
1.2	19·5	13·0 to 21·4 − ±4·2	±21·5
2.1	9·3	6·6 to 12·5 − ±3·0	±32·3
2.2	14·8	10·9 to 26·4 − ±7·7	±52·0
3.1	10·9	4·8 to 13·0 − ±4·1	±37·6
3.2	5·8	2·1 to 7·6 − ±2·7	±46·6
4.0	6·1	3·4 to 15·4 − ±6·0	±98·4

The one group which stands out from the rest is 4.0, courses addressed to disadvantaged students, for which the range of deviation is very wide indeed. It is not surprising that this should be so, for this is the most recent element in the curriculum and is still very much a field for experiment. Nor is there as yet an established public for such courses, as there seems to be for those in the other subject groups; indeed in this field many adult educators are still seeking out a public. (Thus in the literacy campaign there was a period in which many institutions found that their supply of would-be teachers outran their recruitment of students.) So the difference between institutions is much greater for these courses than for those in any other group.

Subject groups 2.2 and 3.2 show a narrower, but still a wide range of variation. In the case of 3.2 this is perhaps to be expected from the somewhat miscellaneous nature of the group, which can include everything from bridge (the subject most frequently mentioned) to astrophysics. The incidence of Group 2.2 may be strongly influenced by the nature of the host institution, as has been suggested above, and also presumably by the availability or otherwise of suitable accommodation and equipment.

Two subject groups, 1.1 and 1.2 in the Survey group – which between them account for 53:1 per cent of the total curriculum – show a surprising consistency of provision over most types of institutions, and two others – 2.1 and 3.1 – a fair degree of consistency. Together these seem to constitute a core curriculum which is common to most institutions. That this should be so is surprising when one considers that adult education institutions are free from any constraints of externally imposed syllabuses and examinations, that they differ widely in structure and philosophy and that their programmes are planned by adult educators many of whom have a considerable degree of autonomy. They can in theory teach what they like, yet three-quarters of their work is in fact basically similar. There seems to be some sort of national consensus that these are the kinds of things that institutions of adult education ought to be offering the public and that there is something wrong if these subjects are not given something like their due place in the programme. And evidently adult educators, on the whole, share or go along with this view. Yet if there is such a national consensus it is difficult to see how it operates, for there is no national organisation or channel of communication through which it can be expressed and no common body of students demanding the common curriculum; in short, no organised or easily identifiable adult education public.

A different interpretation of the situation is that adult educators are influenced not by one large public but by several smaller ones with little communication between them: thus there may be a domestic crafts public, an arts public, a keep-fit public, a sports and games public, a languages public, and so on. So in spite of the fact that adult educators and their institutions are highly idiosyncratic, so that one may seem mainly concerned about sailing or another devoted to drama, they are also aware of their different publics and feel an obligation (if only as a matter of prudence) to give each of them some share of available resources. This is presumably one of the considerations that they have in mind when they talk, as they frequently do, of a 'balanced' programme. If adult educators are in fact dealing not with one public but with several different publics this may in part account for the difficulties which they encounter in trying to generate a sense of common membership and a representative organisation among their students. And it may go some way towards explaining why it is that LEA adult education has never developed a national student body or organisation like, for example, the Workers' Educational Association.

Chapter 7

The capacity for innovation

An assumption which we brought to the research is that adult education is a developing service which has to be flexible in response to emerging and changing needs. Additionally, we assumed that different types of institution would vary in their ability to respond to such needs, that is in their capacity to innovate and develop. But what evidence is there of a general capacity for innovation? Four areas were selected for investigation:

- Was a particular programme more, or less, traditional in content?
- Were many or few new things being attempted?
- How much development work was undertaken?
- Did a head of centre believe innovation to be an important aspect of his work?

Programme analysis

Initially we looked for evidence in programmes. The indicators used were selected in response to the question, what is traditional in adult education programmes – what are the norms? In general, programmes tend to consist of certain staple subjects (mainly in Curriculum Groups 1.1 and 2.1), ungraded courses, evening activities and courses lasting two terms or more; additionally they include very little work for the disadvantaged. Therefore the proportion of non-staple subjects, of graded courses, of daytime activities, of courses shorter than two terms and of courses for the disadvantaged were taken as possible indicators of innovative capacity. They are no more than indicators; it is not claimed that they are necessarily important factors in themselves. And we realise that there are other fields of possible innovation (social activities, clubs and societies, external links, community involvement, etc.) than the directly educational one with which we are here concerned, and that the work of institutions which tend to develop in these directions will not be fully represented in the following analysis. But we have had to work initially with such evidence as is available and measurable, and although we are very far from claiming that only the measurable is real it would be equally absurd to swing to the opposite pole and suggest that the measurable can therefore be ignored; it is also real and has to be accounted for.

The results of this analysis of five indicators of educational innovation are summarised in Table 7.1. The figures are points above and below the median scores of the 131 institutions concerned; they are arrived at by the same process as that described for subject groups in the previous chapter.

Table 7.1 Indicators of innovative capacity: Rank order

Type of institution	No.	(1) 1.1+2.1 courses	(2) 4.0 courses	(3) Graded courses	(4) Daytime courses	(5) Short courses	(6) Educational Innovation Index
Sp. 1	21	—20	+17	+34	+41	+10	+24
2	14	—11	— 6	— 1	—20	+ 3	— 3
3	11	+ 6	—17	+ 1	—41	—17	—16
4	16	+20	—31	—20	— 2	+ 7	—13
FE. 1	15	—16	+12	+14	+14	+22	+16
2	12	+ 3	+10	+ 3	+11	+16	+ 7
Comm. 1	21	+ 3	—14	—20	—31	+10	—12
2	4	—40	+28	—20	+ 7	+ 4	+12
AY 1	9	— 2	+24	—. 6	—16	+ 8	+ 2
2	8	+17	+12	—48	—10	— 3	—13

This table is presented in visual form in the following figures 7.1 to 7.10

Fig. 7.1 *Sp.1*

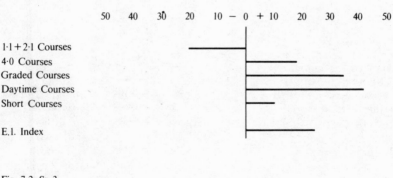

Fig. 7.2 *Sp.2*

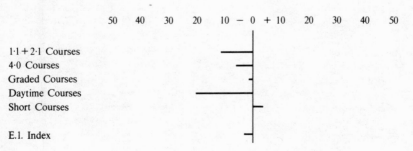

Fig. 7.3 *Sp. 3*

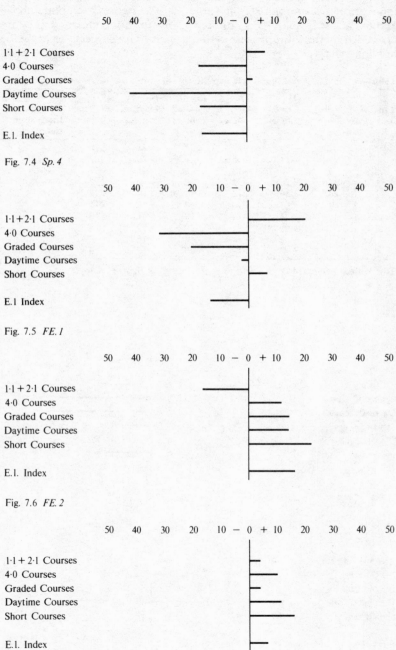

Fig. 7.4 *Sp. 4*

Fig. 7.5 *FE. 1*

Fig. 7.6 *FE. 2*

Fig. 7.7 *Comm. 1*

```
         50   40   30   20   10 — 0 + 10   20   30   40   50

1·1 + 2·1 Courses
4·0 Courses
Graded Courses
Daytime Courses
Short Courses

E.1. Index
```

Fig. 7.8 *Comm. 2*

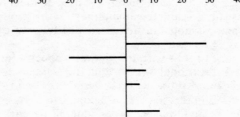

```
         50   40   30   20   10 — 0 + 10   20   30   40   50

1·1 + 2·1 Courses
4·0 Courses
Graded Courses
Daytime Courses
Short Courses

E.1. Index
```

Fig. 7.9 *AY 1*

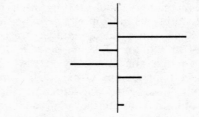

```
         50   40   30   20   10 — 0 + 10   20   30   40   50

1·1 + 2·1 Courses
4·0 Courses
Graded Courses
Daytime Courses
Short Courses

E.1. Index
```

Fig. 7.10 *AY 2*

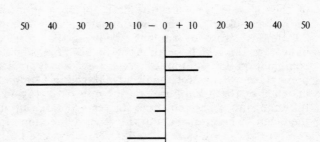

```
         50   40   30   20   10 — 0 + 10   20   30   40   50

1·1 + 2·1 Courses
4·0 Courses
Graded Courses
Daytime Courses
Short Courses

E.1. Index
```

Columns 1 and 2 in Table 7.1 are derived from Table 6.1. Groups 1.1 and 2.1 are largely made up of those courses (domestic crafts and keep fit) which are the traditional staples of adult education and which, therefore, are likely to form a smaller proportion of an innovatory programme; Group 4.0 contains all courses addressed to disadvantaged groups, of which courses addressed to the elderly form a large proportion. Column 3 includes all forms of graded courses in all subjects but excludes 'First Year', 'Beginners', 'Introductory', etc. courses since courses so described are not necessarily the beginning of a graded series. Column 4 includes all courses held in other than the traditional evening period. Column 5 includes all courses less than two terms in length. The 'Educational Innovation Index' is simply the average of columns 1 to 5 with the sign in column 1 reversed.

Urban Community Schools (Comm. 2) planned and fully staffed and equipped as such (not merely existing schools renamed) are relatively new institutions and few in number. Of this group and of AY 1, we had a very small sample, sufficient to justify only one or two simple and obvious observations.

The institutions with the greatest capacity for innovation, as shown by the Educational Innovation Index seem to be Sp. 1, FE. 1 and Comm. 2 and those with the least Sp. 3 and 4, Comm. 1 and AY 2. Innovation in this sense thus belongs, to a considerable extent, to large institutions and to urban areas, and this is clearly to be expected. On the other hand there are urban areas (Sp. 3 and AY 2) as well as rural areas (Sp. and Comm. 1) with a low index; comparison with other members of the same institutional groups suggests that the transition from a predominantly full-time to a predominantly spare-time service may be the decisive factor here. Such staffing differences are less clear-cut in group FE. Institutions in Comm. 1 seem on the whole to be little more innovatory than those (also mainly rural) in Sp. 4; their urban counterparts in Comm. 2 seem on the other hand to be highly innovative, though almost wholly in the direction of work for the disadvantaged (Curriculum Group 4.0). But evidence drawn from programmes is likely to misrepresent the work of community institutions of both types, for they tend to sponsor a wide range of clubs, societies and activities other than classes and these may not be listed in a normal programme and in any case would not be reckoned in the count of classes which provides the basis for programme analysis. This is shown very clearly by the questionnaire (Table 7.2, line 2).

Columns 1 to 5 of Table 7.1 showing the scores on the separate indicators, may well be thought to be more significant than their combination in column 6. We have already remarked upon the dominance of work for the disadvantaged in Comm. 2; this is almost matched by the Adult plus Youth group AY 1 – again urban and with full-time staff. (Though these figures are based upon small samples there can be no doubts about the general direction of interest of these two types of institution.) The difference between full-time and spare-time staffing comes out again in the difference between AY 1 and 2 though the general characteristics of this group of institutions are retained. Substantial numbers of graded courses are found only in Sp. 1 and FE. 1 and, rather less clearly, in FE. 2: these are the institutions which are most concerned with formal teaching and with academic subjects and standards. Daytime courses (column 4) are obviously most frequent in those institutions which can command the use of some premises of their own (Sp. 1). One would expect the provision of daytime courses to be easier in institutions in shared premises than in those using borrowed premises; this seems to be so in the case of FE. 1 and 2 but, very surprisingly, not to be so in the case of Comm. 1. There are not such wide variations in the provision of short courses though here FE. 1 and 2 score highly, followed by Sp. 1 and Comm. 1. The most traditional programmes (column 1) are naturally those of the smaller institutions with spare-time staff (Sp. 4 and AY 2), and the least traditional those of the large, experimental, urban community institutions (Comm. 2).

Interviews: Special enquiry

Given the limitations of programme evidence an attempt was made in connection with interviews to check these findings by asking for a written answer to the following question; those who had not answered by the date of the interview were asked to do so afterwards and return by post.

'Please list below the new things, if any, which you have tried or will be trying during the sessions 1974–75 and 1975–76. These might include such things as: subjects or methods of teaching; layout, timing or location of courses; type of student or potential student; organisations with which you co-operate; ways of running the centre or planning the programme. Please include anything new which you consider is worth recording.'

The question focused the issue of innovation – were many new things being attempted or only a few? – was there an innovative and responsive feel about the centre? Answers were analysed in conjunction with responses to questions in interviews, about the lines of development pursued in recent years. It was to be expected that institutions with a higher capacity to innovate would be concerned with more developments and more 'new things' than those with a lower capacity. The interview was of particular value here in that it gave participants many opportunities to refer to developments which were not recalled by the specific question. It also gave Community School staff a chance to talk about developments with which they could not be credited in programme analysis, such as, for example, student participation in management of the centre, affiliated societies, fund raising, community action, examination courses, etc. The analysis left certain very strong impressions which support the findings so far. The most innovative institutions are to be found in Sp. 1; FE. 1 institutions are highly innovative (though not as high as Sp. 1); Comm. 2 institutions seem to be less innovative than FE. 1 but more innovative than FE. 2 and Sp. 2; and the least innovative are to be found in Sp. 3 and 4. Community institutions seen to have their own characteristic patterns of innovation and development which do not necessarily produce statistics of innovation of the kind that would register in Table 7.1.

Further confirmation of these findings is provided in the replies to the questionnaire. This, it will be remembered, was issued at the very beginning of the research, before our typology of institutions had even been adumbrated. Some 1,500 replies had been received, and these were re-analysed in the light of the typology. This produced a sample of 478 replies which could be clearly and unambiguously assigned to one or other of our institutional types and which were reasonably well distributed between them. We were particularly interested in the responses to the question: What do you see as the main lines of development of your centre? Table 7.2 selects two types of answers to this question, both of which are relevant to our discussion of innovation.

Table 7.2   Types of development

Type of institution	Sp. 1	Sp. 2	Sp. 3	Sp. 4	FE.	Comm. 1	AY 2
No. of respondents	56	73	63	122	45	53	66
1. Percentage describing 'development' in terms of work with disadvantaged groups	54	46	27	7	51	30	42
2. Percentage describing 'development' in terms of clubs, societies, self-supporting groups, etc.	21	30	13	10	27	55	37

(There were insufficient returns to justify any figures for Comm. 2 and AY 1, and there was insufficient evidence in the returns to enable us to make a clear distinction between FE. 1 and 2.)

These figures confirm the position of the large Specialised Institutions and Colleges of Further Education as major providers of courses for disadvantaged groups, and of the Community Schools and Colleges as the major promoters of self-governing and independent groups.

Evidence from interviews supports the contention that the Specialised Institution with its own premises (Sp. 1) is the most innovative and development oriented environment. Typically, heads of centre in this category see innovation as a specific aspect of their role; in contrast very few in any other institutional group do so. All of the following quotations are from interviews in Sp. 1 institutions:

'I find every week there are new ideas, new projects.'
*'Institutions must never stand still or else they die; there is a feeling of
life and excitement – it's the life blood of these places.'*
'If we don't progress we are not educational.'
*'I pride myself and I get my kicks out of being creative, out of being
innovative . . . we've got a lot of firsts in this centre.'*
'I see myself as a catalyst for developing the ideas of others.'
'There is never enough money to fulfil the exciting possibilities.'

This innovative sense is often strong enough to produce a constructive
response in the face of standstills or cuts in budgets. Thus we were told
that 'Even in a no growth situation if you don't put something new in you
don't grow, you die.' For some, however, it was not just a reaction for
the sake of doing 'something new', but the seizing of a development
possibility: 'The lack of money could be a blessing in disguise because it
gives us an opportunity to look at the structure as a whole', or 'to look at
our programmes critically', or 'to reappraise and think'. Again, we were
told, 'It's a good exercise educationally.' These comments should not be
taken to imply that adult educators approve of expenditure cuts – they
are merely identifying an advantage to set against the many
disadvantageous consequences of financial stringency; as one interviewee observed if you take cut-backs far enough 'the effect would be to
take away the creativity which is so essential to adult education'.

Possible explanations of differences in capacity for innovation

How are differences in innovative capacity and in attitudes to
innovation to be explained? In referring to the results of programme
analysis it was suggested that such variables as size, urban environment
and full-time staffing might provide explanations. Moreover, the
limited size of adult education institutions typically permits a head of
centre to have a decisive influence. These possible explanations can be
dealt with under three main headings, the individual, the organisation
and the environment.

The individual

There is a strong individualistic tradition in research into innovative
behaviour. Although we did not set out to test for differences in
individual characteristics we did assume that adult education institutions are generally small enough for the individual head of centre to
have a strong influence on organisational performance – even the
largest institutions, with 10,000 or more enrolments, have a full-time
staff of less than twenty (though they may have several hundred spare-
time teachers) – and this, of course, is quite exceptional. In Chapter 8 it
is suggested that adult educators may be attracted to Specialised
Institutions because of the autonomy in the role – they can be 'Mr.

Adult Education'. It is arguable that this possibility for independent action, for strongly influencing the development of an institution, attracts individuals with certain personality characteristics related to self-confidence and creativity but we have not tested for these. However, what is certain is that in the Specialised Institution the individual head of centre uses his autonomy to be innovative, particularly in large institutions; whatever relevant personality characteristics he may possess, it is the opportunity present in the work situation which permits him to exercise these. It is significant here that there is a very marked difference in innovative capacity between large Specialised Institutions (Sp. 1) and medium-sized institutions (Sp. 2); in the latter situation staff do not demonstrate the same innovative behaviour although they have, in theory, a comparable autonomy. In practice, however, that autonomy is limited by their lack of any teaching accommodation of their own.

The organisation

1. Size and specialisation

Does the explanation for these differences in capacity for innovation lie in difference of size and related staffing levels? In Table 7.3 size has been measured by the number of courses plus the number of affiliated societies (the latter have been included because they are often such a large part of total provision in Community Schools). Under staffing only those with some organising responsibility have been included. In determining full-time equivalents a part-time appointment has been treated as a half-time commitment; the only exception to this is in those Community Schools which have both adult and youth tutors, or two appointments of senior tutor and tutor covering these two areas, in which case the school has been credited with the equivalent of one full-time appointment in the adult work. A spare-time appointment has

Table 7.3   Size and staffing of institutions

Type of institution	(1) Average size (number of courses and affiliated societies)	(2) Average no. of full-time organising staff (or equivalent)	(3) Average no. of courses per full-time member of staff (1 $\div$ 2)
Sp. 1	390	6:5	60
2	100	1:7	59
3	62	0:4	155
4	c. 30*	0:4	75
FE. 1	315	6:5	48
2	93	1:1	85
Comm. 1	86	1:4	61
2	138	6:0	23
AY 1	200	4:4	45
2	53	0:4	133

* only an approximate figure can be given for programmes typically include all activities for an area, which will consist of several centres.

been assessed on the basis of the number of sessions worked; for example, three evenings is equivalent to 3/10 of a full-time appointment (assuming a ten-session week). Such measurements can only be approximate, nevertheless they are adequate for our purposes.

The basic assumption is that the more staff there are the more likely they will be to specialise in aspects of the work, for example, by geographical area, by subject, or by type of student. Indeed in some cases specialised appointments of these kinds are made, for example, tutor for craft subjects, or for the disadvantaged. Whether there are specialised appointments or not, however, does not determine the degree of specialisation – it is clear from interviews that staff do specialise, where staffing levels permit, in those aspects of the work, which are in line with their own interests and abilities. Whether formal or informal, specialisation leads individuals to conduct search activities in their area of interest; such activities lead to the identification of innovation and development possibilities.

Undoubtedly the largest institutions, Sp. 1 and FE. 1, are the most innovative. However, the number of full-time staff (6·5), and the consequent specialisation, does not appear to be an adequate explanation because, the urban Community Schools (Comm. 2), though having approximately the same number of staff (6) as Sp. 1 and FE. 1, seem to show in certain respects a lower capacity for innovation. This may be the misleading effect of a small sample or of the newness of these institutions, most of which have hardly had time to realise their full potential. Or a partial explanation may lie in the observation that '. . . increased size expands the possibilities for interacting with the environment . . . since additional clients multiply the number of interested outsiders making their special demands'.[1] Thus it could be argued that urban Community Schools (Comm. 2) are less innovative than institutions in either the Sp. 1 or FE. 1 categories because they have much smaller adult education programmes – they have fewer opportunities for interacting with their environment because they have fewer students. It should be noted, however, that size in adult education is to some extent a matter of choice. Therefore, with a given level of staffing, and within the limitations of budgets and the willingness of students to attend, an institution can have X or X+50 or X+100 students; in this context it is relevant that institutions with similar staffing in both categories Sp. 1 and FE. 1 do vary markedly in size of programme. There is also a marked difference in the average number of courses and affiliated societies per full-time member of staff in different kinds of institution (Table 7.3, column 3); urban Community Schools have a low average (23) compared with Sp. 1 (60) and FE. 1 (48). [The reader should be wary of accepting the figures as a measure of relative productivity because they are themselves based on another calculation (column 2) and take no account of other aspects of work than the maintenance of a programme of courses and affiliated groups; nevertheless the difference is so marked as to be worthy of note. The other obvious contrast in column 3 is between institutions with spare-time staff, Sp. 3 and AY 2, and the rest. Here the calculation in column 2 is probably most suspect; but there can be no doubt that services with mainly spare-time appointments do appear to be seriously under-staffed, particularly in urban areas. The relatively low figure for Sp. 4 may reflect the difficulties of work in a rural environment but is also open to the most doubt because of the added problem of calculating the size of the programme (see footnote, Table 7.3).]

Size of programme is, however, not the only factor influencing the range of contacts with the environment. Another may be the tendency either to concentrate the programme in one set of buildings or to disperse it through many. We found that it was not uncommon for institutions in groups Sp. 1 and FE. 1 to be working in anything from thirty to sixty locations outside the main centre or college, and we were often told that this was inevitable if they were to meet the needs of their area and maintain a large and varied programme. The community institutions (Comm. 1 and 2) tend to use fewer outside premises than other kinds of institution of comparable size. Rural Community Schools use more, perhaps because of difficulties of transport, than do the urban and suburban ones: in these a usual assumption seems to be that 'everything goes on in the campus'.

It may well be that such observations are premature and that urban Community Schools need more time to establish themselves in a community role. *'I think it is inevitable that their first priority should be to establish credibility with the school staff which may have been suspicious of community education and development. . . . So I think that if I were in their shoes I would be doing the same thing: I would have made sure that the home base was well established.'* Moreover if such excellent buildings and equipment are provided and if there is felt to be an obligation to 'maximise their use' so as to justify capital expenditure, why use inferior premises elsewhere? One answer, given the undoubtedly strengthening desire to serve a wider community, may lie in the location of many of these otherwise excellent premises: they have had to be built where there was a considerable acreage of land available. Hence the frequency of such comments as 'We are inconveniently placed on the edge of town'; 'The school is inaccessible'; 'You have to be pretty well motivated to walk here, it's two miles from the town centre.' In these circumstances it might be anticipated that they would tend to operate more of their activities in locations having greater convenience for students. Some rural Community Schools have, of course, taken the alternative step of providing a bus service, though this is a declining practice.

There is no doubt of the desire of adult educators in Community Schools and Colleges to work in outside locations and extend their contacts in the community. In this their school base and their range of affiliated organisations may give them as yet not fully exploited sources of strength which other institutions lack.

'Parents are your first link between the community and the College; they are parents with an active interest in the education of their child but they are also adults with their own particular problems and needs and contributions to make. We concentrate initially on the parental response but the ramifications towards adult education are important.'
'It's only in this sort of set-up that you can really make an impact on people's lives through the whole spectrum of their activities, through clubs and societies and social events and hopefully reaching out through things like community primary schools into the communities in which they actually live.'

There is one other way in which Community Schools seem to be more open to their environment – it is clear from the diaries which they kept that heads of centre in these institutions have many more contacts with individuals and groups outside of the organisation and of the education service than those operating in Specialised Institutions and Colleges of Further Education. This must offset the tendency which Community Schools have to mount their programmes within the institution and to have smaller programmes.

2. *The control of premises*

In treating both Sp. 1 and FE. 1 as institutions having a high innovative capacity no attempt has so far been made to explain the marked differences between them – the former has significantly more innovative capacity than the latter although both have broadly comparable urban environments and staffing arrangements and are about the same size. The explanation of this difference probably lies in another organ- isational characteristic – institutions in category Sp. 1 have some teaching premises of their own whereas almost all FE. 1 institutions have to share accommodation with the other college departments. The consequence of this is reflected in the index of daytime activities (Table 7.1, column 4); Sp. 1 institutions have a very much higher index of daytime activities than any other kind of institution. It is to be expected, therefore, that they will be more innovative than other institutions which either have to share or borrow premises; access to your own daytime accommodation permits of so much development particularly in the area of disadvantaged work, for example with the elderly and the handicapped.

Possession of premises can be seen as enhancing the autonomy of the adult educator – thus it is part of the attraction of the role in Specialised Institutions. It not only permits of greater experimentation but allows the practitioner to create an adult environment unaffected by the consequence of school or college use in the shape of inappropriate regulations, furnishings or equipment – to create a place with a distinctive atmosphere or ethos.

'It seems to me that there you get a dimension which is missing in the school. You get a feeling that this is a place to which adults go, a place

which is truly adult where adults can behave as adults do behave. With the best will in the world on the part of the headmaster, on the part of the staff, I still have to go into a . . . school or college where this sense of an adult community . . . actually exists.'

'A college . . . has nothing like the ethos which you can create in an adult education centre, it's quite different. . . . When people go into a college situation . . . they feel that it is formalised. Your main concern in a separate adult education set-up is that . . . it's got to be very warm and welcoming, very caring and personal . . . and very efficiently run.'

'. . . until we have a situation where adult education is an educational service in it own right with purpose-built or purpose-adapted premises, full-time staff and technical and administrative back-up . . . anything less than this seems to me to have enormous failings . . .'

The environment

So far it can probably be concluded that the attitude to innovation and the organisational autonomy of the individual adult educator are important but perhaps not the most important determinants of innovative behaviour. Of greater significance seem to be staffing levels and size of programme. In the case of institutions with the greatest innovative capacity, Sp. 1, the explanation also partly lies in them having some premises of their own.

A further critical determinant is likely to be the environment of a centre – the socio-economic mix of its catchment population, its density, etc. Although we abandoned any attempt to measure environmental variability (see Ch. 4) it has to be acknowledged that broadly urban situations, as opposed to rural ones, offer many more opportunities for innovation because of their greater density and heterogeneity of population. Thus an urban environment provides, for example, critical masses of students requiring a particular subject, or more than one grade of activity in a subject, or an activity for a specific type of handicapped person. It seems likely, however, that environment is less important than staffing level, because both rural (Sp. 4) and urban (Sp. 3) institutions with spare-time staff show comparably low innovative capacities. The critical determinant here appears to be the level of staffing; the spare-timer with little time, little support and often no opportunity to specialise, is in most cases unable to demonstrate much innovative behaviour. Comparable urban environments relate in much the same way to different innovative capacities of institutions in categories Sp. 1, FE. and Com.; again the pattern and level of staffing seems to be the decisive factor.

The effect of student participation The critical link between organisation and environment would appear to be the capacity to identify the opportunities present and to respond to them, that is the degree of openness of an institution – the capacity and willingness to conduct search activities, to develop links which lead to the identification of particular needs. It has been observed that '. . . any social organisation seeking innovation must make itself vulnerable by opening channels of communication and influence to its environment'.[1] It has already been established that Community Schools, for example, have fewer outside locations and fewer students than Sp. 1 or FE. 1 institutions and therefore fewer opportunities for interacting with the environment. On the other hand Community Schools have many more contacts with individuals and groups outside of the centre. Again, they typically have a communication network based on their college council or adult association or management council, etc. made up of users and others. Is there any evidence that contacts of this kind lead to more innovative programmes? There were mixed views on this in the interviews; for example:

'I need the support of the users to get at the non-users – they provide, for example, free transport for the handicapped.'
'They voluntarily agreed to take a cut in their resources, a 5 per cent reduction, in order to finance adult literacy work, showing that although it was against their own interests to do this they were willing to see a need outside of their own members and able to respond to it.'
Or, on the other hand:
'The trouble is that they reflect the views of our existing students and not those outside.'
'If the programme were determined by those who are willing and able to pay the fees it would be oriented towards . . . their interests.'

It is possible to test for the effect of student participation in programme planning by identifying in Comm. 1 (all with some formally structured participation) those institutions in which interviewees claimed that students had a major influence on programme and those in which it was maintained they had little influence. These institutions were then ranked according to their Educational Innovation Index (Table 7.1, column 6). The result of the comparison is very marked; a major student influence in programme planning is equated with a lower index. Of the institutions listed only one claiming that students exercised a major influence figures is in the top half of the list. Such a test, applied to a relatively small number of institutions, can be no more than an indicator of the possible effect of student participation on innovation. Nevertheless, the contrast was most marked and suggests the need for further research.

Such a finding is in line with views sometimes expressed by senior officers who are aware of the dangers inherent in student participation in programme planning:

'It could orientate the programmes towards the interests of those who are already in adult education and so ignore the interests of those who have real needs in Russell terms – it stops missionary work in that area. The way to counter this is to retain some funds centrally, to by-pass

them in setting up, for example, courses in local hospitals.'
'The student committees have nothing to do with people who don't use the Community Schools and we can't allow that.'

Or, as it was put by an experienced practitioner:

'Do you think that the professional is more likely to be concerned with the educationally or economically underprivileged than is the lay member of, say a students' council?'
'No, I don't think that. I think that the professional is better placed. I'll put it in personal terms – at the risk of seeming arrogant. I am better placed because of my knowledge and field work to have a wide view of the needs of the community . . . than are most lay people, and therefore I'm in a position to advise a lay group. Though that, of course, is a delicate operation.'

The innovatory capacity of particular centres

So far we have only been concerned with categories of institution. Further evidence as to causation may be extracted by looking at particular centres whose Education Innovation Index is very much higher than others in the same category or in the same local authority. Two such examples occur in Groups Sp. 3 and Sp. 4. One institution in each category has an Education Innovation Index half as high again as any other in the same group so that their immediate comparators are institutions with full-time staff in Sp. 2 and FE. 2. They have small programmes and spare-time staffing so the explanation does not lie in the area of size and specialisation. Nor is there anything atypical about their environment. The researcher is then forced back to explanations centred on the individual and there is a critical way in which the two heads of centre differ from the others in their particular categories – though they are both spare-time adult educators they do not have a full-time job and, additionally, they do much of their work during the day and have control of some daytime accommodation. In consequence they tend to spend much more time on their work than they are paid for and have a very much higher than average daytime programme of activities.

These idiosyncratic examples underline the importance of the amount of time available to do the job; the practitioners concerned are nearer to part-time workers by our definition but without the distractions of other paid employment. Both, in effect, specialise in adult education and would like to work full-time in that field. Alongside this the existence of some own accommodation is an important factor. The effect of the latter is also apparent in one exceptional institution in AY2 which has an Education Innovation Index over half as high again as any other centre in the same category or in the same local authority; the same spare-time staffing arrangements and comparable environments indicate that explanations do not lie in those areas. In this instance the head of centre does have another full-time job which probably explains why, although the Education Innovation Index is high for its category, it is lower than for the two examples discussed above in Groups Sp. 3 and 4. The residual explanation is apparently the control of some accommodation which permits of a relatively high number of daytime activities; administrative cover for these aspects of the programme is achieved by concentrating all of the part-time clerical assistance into the day.

These examples assist in focusing the major determinants of differences in innovative capacity. They suggest that where personal circumstances permit a spare-time head of centre to 'specialise' in adult education and where there is control over premises, then a sense of commitment is generated and there is a very marked rise in innovatory capacity. The former finding links with the view expressed earlier that the opportunities for staff specialisation are probably more important than other determinants; though specialisation in the use of time is of a different order from specialisation by, say, subject or area, it is in our view merely an earlier step in the same process. In accounting for the differences between Sp. 1 and FE. 1 we focused on control over premises as an important determinant which links very well with the finding from the idiosyncratic examples. It is, therefore, in the combination of a full-time service, opportunities for staff specialisation, and the control over accommodation that much of the explanation for innovatory capacity must lie. Environment, autonomy and attitude to innovation are also contributory factors.

The importance of a supportive framework

Two further exceptional examples help to identify a further determinant. In the top six institutions in terms of their Educational Innovation Index there are four large Specialised Institutions (Sp. 1), with programmes of approximately 500 classes, and two Colleges of Further Education, in which adult education does not have departmental status, with only 112 and 67 classes respectively. Two such remarkable exceptions call for comment; size, specialisation and environment do not apparently provide an explanation. There is, however, one identifiable difference with other institutions in category FE. 1, they both have very supportive principals, one of whom has been a full-time head of an adult institute. Both principals are very active in the adult programme of their colleges either as teachers, as the evening 'adult tutor on duty', or in visiting classes. This suggests an important variable which we have not yet considered, the attitude of individuals in positions of authority who can strongly influence the organisational environment in which adult educators work. We have established elsewhere that in Colleges of Further Education the supportive and protective principal can be vital to adult education; in Community Schools the attitude of Principals tends to be less supportive (Ch. 8). Given the traditional independence of the school or college the attitude of the head or principal is likely to be a critical factor in encouraging or discouraging innovation.

In the Specialised Institution it will be the attitude of senior officers at county or city hall which is important. How much independence of action do they allow to their heads of centre and how much support do they provide? The autonomy usually claimed by heads of Specialised Institutions is reflected in the following observations by senior officers:

'They have a lot of independence.'
'They have a very free rein to develop their work in their own image.'
'We recognise our principals as being professional staff of some experience and status who should be entitled to make decisions that they think appropriate locally.'

In terms of protection senior officers responsible tend to see their job in terms of 'protecting adult education from elected members', and in trying to obtain more resources, particularly full-time staff, for adult education.

The importance of a supportive Local Education Authority cannot be over-emphasised. One way in which senior officers provide protection is to stress in their negotiations with committees the social value of adult education. To the extent that they can defend the budget and can mount support for particular aspects of the programme they assist the head of centre in his efforts to develop his programme. Additionally, if the local authority can be persuaded to provide adequate administrative and clerical support at centre level this frees the practitioner for development aspects of his role in terms of the educational content of courses, strengthening contacts with students, and conducting search activities in the community. If, on the other hand, the local authority chooses to starve the service of adequate funds, leaves it much understaffed, applies very restrictive fee and enrolment regulations, and generally demonstrates its low status, then it must expect to stifle initiative. It will get the service it deserves: unimaginative and with little capacity for innovation and development.

Reference

1. **Baldridge, J. V.**, (1975) in **Baldridge and Deal, T. E.**, *Managing Change in Educational Organisations*, California, p. 163.

Chapter 8

Adult educators: problems and job satisfactions

This chapter will be concerned primarily with the job satisfactions of adult educators working in Specialised Institutions with full-time appointments (Sp. 1 and 2), in Colleges of Further Education (FE. 1 and 2), and in Community Schools and Colleges (Comm. 1 and 2). A secondary concern will be their personal characteristics and career profiles (Tables 8.1 and 8.2). The figures in these tables are of course based upon what interviewees told us about themselves and their jobs and no attempt has been made to check this information. Though we are here concerned mainly with full-time and part-time appointments the response of spare-time staff in Specialised Institutions (Sp. 3 and 4) will also be referred to where appropriate; the interview sample was too small to permit us to do this for institutions in Category AY.

Table 8.1   Personal characteristics of adult educators

Type of institution	(No.)	Male (%)	Av. age (years)	Av. length of time in present post (years)	Trained teacher (%)	Graduate (%)	Diploma in adult education (%)
Sp. 1 and 2	(26)	78	42	5	59	40·7	22
FE. 1 and 2	(20)	100	44·5	5·4	80	35	10
Comm. 1 and 2	(20)	84	42·5	5·4	74	36·8	10·5
All groups	(66)	87·3	43·7	5·3	71	37·5	14·2

Table 8.2   Career routes of adult educators

Type of institution	(No.)	Spare-time adult teaching (%)	Spare-time head of centre (%)	Youth work (%)
Sp. 1 and 2	(26)	41	52	15
FE. 1 and 2	(20)	40	30	10
Comm. 1 and 2	(20)	10	20	47
All groups	(66)	30·3	34	24

In marked contrast to the part-time adult teaching role the organising role in adult education is a male preserve – there are probably some nine male organisers to every female. Organisers are typically in early middle age (average forty-three years) and have been in the same post for approximately five years. This surprised us: we had expected to find evidence suggesting a quite rapid turnover of staff, particularly in Community Schools. It should be remembered, however, that we are dealing only with the few who have overall responsibility for a centre programme and that there is likely to be a more rapid turnover of the more junior members of staff.

Over 70 per cent are trained teachers and roughly the same percentage have had full-time teaching experience in schools; only 15 per cent have a specific qualification in adult education. Rather more than a third are graduates, though very few have a higher degree. As between types of institution there are fewer trained teachers in Specialised Institutions than in the other categories, but more graduates and considerably more with a qualification in adult education. The figure for trained teachers in Colleges of Further Education seemed to us surprisingly high for it is usually assumed that college staff have a more varied background, often in industry or commerce, than school teachers. What seems likely is that the adult educator in a College of Further Education is normally drawn from those with a Liberal Studies, Arts or Physical Education rather than an Industry or Commerce background and so will tend to have been trained as a teacher. In developing an adult education career the majority have taken the obvious route via adult teaching and/or the spare-time headship of a centre to a full-time or part-time appointment. This is the norm for organisers working in Specialised Institutions or Colleges of Further Education. Community Schools present a sharp contrast to this, for nearly half of the adult educators in these institutions have experience not in adult education but in youth work.

Typically, therefore, adult educators are experienced either in teaching or in youth work and are in the middle stage of their careers; only 15 per cent have had much experience outside of these special areas of professional competence, though about 20 per cent have had experience of teaching outside schools and colleges, e.g. overseas, in H.M. Forces, the Workers' Educational Association, prisons, etc.

What possibilities for career development do they see? Most were either content to stay in their present post or did not identify any specific development. There was a marked contrast in response, however, in Specialised Institutions compared with Community Schools and Colleges of Further Education; in the former over one in three were uncertain about career development and failed to identify any possibilities: 'I'm not clear', 'I'm not sure where it leads', were typical responses. Sometimes this was seen as clearly related to the size of most adult education institutions:

'There is precious little career development, that is quite clear; wherever you go in the country it just isn't there. And it perhaps isn't there because we are one-man outfits. A centre, you see, it's one man. It's rather like the Religious Education Department in a school: you

become Head of Department in your first year and then you are finished.'

In contrast, in Community Schools and Colleges of Further Education very few expressed uncertainty seemingly because the more comprehensive educational provision of these institutions offers opportunities for promotion within the system; typical references were to a 'more senior role' or to a 'head of department' post.

Autonomy

Though the adult educator in a Specialised Institution sometimes complains of a lack of career opportunities he will, almost without exception, point to the very positive job satisfaction resulting from the autonomy which he typically experiences in the role. About 60 per cent of full-time staff, and almost a half of spare-time centre heads, indicated that in practice they did not have a boss, and nearly all saw themselves as autonomous within the authority's regulations. For the great majority of full-time adult educators this was undoubtedly an important source of job satisfaction:

'I like my independence.'
'I'm the boss, I run my own show.'
'We have the structure, we have the regulations, but by and large our employers allow us a lot of autonomy.'
'I expect officers of the authority to have faith in me and my team, to back that faith with resources and to give us near to total flexibility to administer these resources, and I get it.'

Further evidence as to the value they place on autonomy can be gleaned from their attitude to other kinds of institution. Though they often showed an understanding of the advantages of working in Colleges of Further Education and Community Schools in terms of their resources there was also a marked awareness of the limitation of autonomy entailed:

'The adult educators are always subordinate to someone else.'
'We would not be keen because we have people with ideas and we like to implement them without having to go to someone a little higher up the hierarchy to ask, can we do this?'

The value which they place on their freedom is reflected in such comments as:

'People who are happy in their work are going to perform better and I think people in independent centres are much happier because they have more autonomy . . . and they can mould their own programmes.'
'I see and I have seen from the moment I was appointed that one of my most important roles would be the development of a philosophy for the

Institution, and that this would involve the development and co-ordination of staff.'

Occasionally, however, a head of centre would complain of the isolation which is inherent in this autonomy:

'I am my own boss but we are cut off as though we existed on an island . . . I need support and advice from the office.'
'I don't think that people who haven't worked in this way fully realise what a handicap it can be not only to work by yourself but to work at times when most people are free, to come out in the evening, to come out at weekends.'

Such observations seem to be related to the length of time in this kind of post – it is the relative newcomer to the role who sometimes experiences his freedom as uncertainty and consequently feels in need of support.

Adult educators working in other institutional settings are not unaware of the attractions of the specialised service. Thus, organisers working in Colleges of Further Education with experience of working in a Specialised Institution generally expressed a preference for the latter in terms of its 'autonomy' or 'a programme with an individual style', or 'an identity of its own'; in Community Schools several of those interviewed, though without experience in Specialised Institutions, expressed approval of them in similar terms. No one operating in a Specialised Centre stated a preference for working in either a Community School or a College of Further Education.

The view that the adult educator in multi-purpose institutions has less autonomy is supported by the fact that in both Colleges of Further Education and Community Schools the principal or head teacher or warden of the institution was typically identified as the boss; in both situations less than a third claimed a large measure of self-determination. Such a response was to be anticipated given the overall responsibility which the principal has for adult education within the institution. The physical presence of a boss and the consequent loss of final responsibility seems to make local authority regulations about numbers and fees more irksome; certainly, for example, it may be more difficult to conceal any circumvention of such regulations in a College of Further Education than in a Specialised Institution. Thus it was observed that, 'The authority is insensitive about fee structures', and that, 'The regulations are too watertight'. Another interviewee pointed to the need to find 'a respectable deviousness' in response to restrictive regulations.

Administrative and financial constraints

Despite his autonomy there are constraints in the Specialised Institute role which produce conflict. Most frequently referred to is the clash between the administrative demands of the job and the desire to spend more time in the educational aspects of the work; it is the conflict which the Russell Report referred to between routine clerical duties and 'work relating to the nature and quality of the teaching and the supervision and development of staff which are fundamental to it' (para. 358). In this context over half complained of a lack of clerical and other ancillary support staff; even in larger establishments, with seemingly relatively generous staffing (Sp. 1), the difficulties were often expressed. The following quotations are taken from both Sp. 1 and 2:

'I'm head of centre, caretaker, canteen assistant, anything that needs to be done at the time I do.'
'I spend too much time on administration.'
'I'm nothing more than a caretaker.'
'I spend half my time trying to find accommodation.'
'I'm just centre-bound with our staffing.'

These constraints are of course felt even more keenly by the spare-time adult educators in Categories Sp. 3 and 4, who often have to spend nearly all their time upon inescapable clerical duties:

'The main responsibility is obviously administration. Most of the tasks are pretty menial; collecting money, issuing receipts, making sure registers are up to date, ordering equipment, that sort of thing. There's nothing difficult about the job but I find I'm sitting at my desk at home doing pay claims, etc., and it does take time.'
'There's a great deal of run-of-the-mill clerical and treasury work; collecting money, banking the money and making sure that the money adds up. . . . There's no clerical assistance – except that my wife is an unpaid clerical assistant. A great deal of the work has to be done at home because people ring you up at home, and therefore I keep most of the records at home.'

When asked to identify those aspects of their job on which they would like to spend more time the answers of interviewees in full-time posts were invariably related to the leadership aspects of the role and tended to fall into two broad areas – in the community making contacts or doing research into areas of need; in the centre making contact with teachers and students. (Similar views were sometimes expressed in Colleges of Further Education and Community Schools though, as will be demonstrated shortly, the administrative – leadership conflict is not felt so keenly there.)

'To do basic research on disadvantaged groups.'
'Making contacts with outside groups, but I'm just centre-bound.'
'With my tutors discussing content, method and introducing new ideas.'
'A lot more time helping and advising students.'

Would any extra time created by more adequate staffing arrangements be spent on such activities? As one Specialised Institute principal observed, 'I've known lots of adult educators who've said I'd love to spend more time in classes but I suspect most people organise themselves to do the things that they can do and they don't do the things that they don't want to do.' It is possible that some adult educators, like some headmasters, become 'lost in the embrace of the office';[1] they do the things which they find easier, avoid doing things which are more troublesome. As Burnham has observed, 'It is tempting to seek the quiet life, to avoid the dilemmas of leadership, by a retreat into "busy-work" . . .'.[2] What can be said with confidence is that in Specialised Institutions where there are either full-time administrative/clerical staff or other full-time organising/teaching staff the development of teacher training and/or teacher supervision is much more frequently identified (79 per cent) than in centres without such staffing arrangements (38 per cent). Whether the principals themselves are actually spending more time on such activities, or ensuring that members of their staff do so, is not clear. However, one result of providing full-time support staff would undoubtedly appear to be that the educational aspects of the work are given much greater emphasis. In Colleges of Further Education a similar difference exists; where adult education has departmental status and where, therefore, there is more than one member of staff and usually full-time clerical support, teacher training or supervision are developments referred to more frequently (66 per cent) than where adult education does not have departmental status (45 per cent). The same test cannot be applied to Community Schools because the development of training or supervision is rarely mentioned.

Any tendency for adult educators to stress the administrative aspects of their role may be reinforced by the expectations of their employers. As one principal of a Specialised Institution observed, 'The next group of principals should be accountants not educationalists; this is not a joke but a definite trend, there is no one at County Hall who has ever been a principal and they don't know the consequences of their actions.' The inadequacy implied in this comment is undoubtedly felt by many for one in three indicated a need for further training in 'administration' or 'management'. Another principal spoke for many when he observed that, 'One of the problems with adult education, in fact with education all through, is that one minute you're in the classroom, the next you're in the management role and typically you've had no training.' In Colleges of Further Education the same situation obtains, one in three identified a need for training in management or administration; in Community Schools it is mentioned much less frequently.

It was implied above that some authorities have acknowledged the need to separate the two aspects of the role by appointing, in major specialised centres, full-time administrative or clerical officers. Others, though aware that heads of centre 'don't get much administrative support . . . they're doing the administrative rather than the educational work', have done too little. Therefore in many authorities the position remains as it was described in the Russell Report: 'Over the years, many adult education principals have carried a quite unjustifiable load of routine clerical work which, ultimately, is undertaken at the expense of the educational supervision of the courses for which they are responsible' (para. 381). There has apparently been little change and Local Education Authorities, far from being seen as supportive, are often experienced as creators of obstacles through their regulations concerning enrolment and attendance. The difficulties these create are frequently identified in both questionnaire and interview; they help to engender a feeling of insecurity which is further exacerbated by some local authorities who have, particularly in recent years – not surprisingly in the light of their financial difficulties – created a climate of uncertainty about the money available for adult education:

'It causes me endless concern and frustration because I like to know what my budget is and then I can plan.'
'There is a lack of stability, I am uncertain what I can spend.'

Sometimes the notification of a cut in budget is not only delayed but comes after the head of centre has completed his programme planning and, in some cases, after the programme is printed. This administrative insensitivity, coupled with a typical lack of consultation over student fee increases, produces a great deal of justifiable frustration and anger among heads of centre.

Do adult educators in Community Schools and Colleges of Further Education feel the same constraints as those working in Specialised Institutions? In both situations the administrative–educational conflict is much less apparent. In Community Schools the problem is with caretaking rather than clerical support whereas in Colleges of Further Education the difficulties are typically of the 'I am increasingly becoming more of a clerk' kind. The explanation for this difference may lie in the fact that in Colleges of Further Education there is a caretaking establishment related to a standard three-session day (morning, afternoon, evening) whereas in Community Schools there is typically an establishment based on a two-session school day, plus a little extra. Several Community School headmasters also identified the caretaking problem and would endorse the view of one of them that 'the community school must be properly staffed for that purpose'.

A universal constraint on adult education at the present time is lack of finance. This is very keenly felt by most practitioners working in both Specialised Institutions and Colleges of Further Education; however, there is a difference of response within these categories because it is in the large institutions (Sp. 1 and FE. 1) that the complaints are most vociferous. In Community Schools finance, though still an important problem, was mentioned less frequently. As most Community Schools have similarly sized programmes to both Sp. 2 and FE. 2 it can probably be concluded that finance is a problem related in some way to size – that is, in general the bigger the programme, and therefore the budget, the more the lack of finance is experienced as a constraint. It seems that the larger the programme the more the organiser becomes aware of development possibilities; more accurately we should probably refer to the organis*ers* because in institutions with large programmes more than one person will be engaged in development and it is more likely, therefore, that new opportunities will be sought out and explored. In this context the responses of spare-time principals in a specialised service are relevant for, in general, they have small programmes and little time to seek out new opportunities; probably in consequence they complain much less frequently of a lack of finance than any other category of adult educator.

A further administrative constraint, to which only passing reference has been made, is local authority regulations about enrolment numbers. It is usually necessary to have twelve or fifteen students before a class can be run though this may be ameliorated by averaging arrangements or by net budgeting. Where it is not, these regulations are usually complained of though they have often been accepted as part of the framework within which adult educators have to operate; they have therefore developed their own ways of bending the rules to fit their concept of what is desirable. But such regulations are still a serious discouragement to experiment and innovation.

'If you're going to get out into experimental or difficult areas of work you've got to accept the fact that it's going to be expensive and that you're going to have low numbers to begin with.'

'People feel that if they choose to do something a bit unusual it's very likely that they won't get numbers, therefore it's very likely that it won't get started, so what's the point of going in the first place ... I mean it's a bit like going to the pictures: you think shall I go to the pictures tonight? But if I go to the pictures and there aren't enough people there they'll just send us all home. So you don't go.'

There seems to be a general interest in and approval of averaging schemes which permit the head of centre some discretion – minimum enrolment numbers are an unnecessary and frustrating constraint. Net budgeting is another, much talked about, method of permitting a discretionary element at centre level but it is, as one senior officer remarked, 'double edged', and does not always have the desired effect: 'It is both an instrument of greater flexibility and a way of preventing over-spending – I don't see people leaping in to transfer money from traditional work into newer ways of working; they are more anxious not to overspend than to exploit the opportunities it offers.' (The basic principle of net budgeting is that the adult educator is allowed to spend a net amount which is the difference between a total sum allocated and an estimated sum for fees paid by students.)

Problems of sharing, borrowing and status

Burton Clark stressed a feature of adult education organisations which he believed helped to explain feelings of insecurity and and lack of status among adult educators in California: 'They are nearly always dependent rather than independent, located within large organisations that are mainly concerned with other tasks.'[3] If such problems exist here they are likely to be of greater significance inside dual or multi-purpose institutions than in Specialised Institutions where there is sometimes at least some teaching accommodation for adult education use only. In this context full-time adult educators in Specialised Institutions without any premises of their own complained of difficulties of borrowing school accommodation three times as often as those with some premises:

'I have no territory of my own, therefore politically I have less weight.'
'If there is a conflict I lose.'
'The school at times have put every obstacle they could in our way.'
'With caretakers you can't win . . . they tell me they are employed by the school and that they put up tables as an act of goodwill but they're damned if they're going to take them down.'
'Some of our worst enemies are school teachers . . . they do not see adult education as education.'

There were also frequently quoted problems of storage: 'We live like moles'; 'My typical tutor is like a travelling tinker'. Several also pointed to the ambiguity of the policy about borrowing arrangements and would welcome a clarification of the situation; there was, however, little support for an edict from the Director of Education because of the possible backlash effect. Though officers at County Hall often expressed awareness of the problem, appropriate action has not followed: 'The principals would like a statement from the Director about the dual use of premises . . . it concerns them greatly', one observed. Another commented that 'adult education is not accorded the respect due to it, the adult education chap is small fry, aggravating and upsetting what is going on in the school – there is a lack of appreciation and understanding at school and area level.'

Similar problems of access to accommodation and a lack of status seem to be even more acute in Colleges of Further Education; both questionnaire and interview identify them as important areas of difficulty. Accommodation difficulties are not confined to the college itself for particularly in institutions with large adult education programmes there is both a need, and frequently a commitment, to go outside of the institution to borrow school premises; where this occurs the same difficulties experienced by organisers operating from a specialised base are often complained of:

'Schools are our biggest problem where the heads can make it very difficult.'

'Adult education is not always welcome in schools, sometimes I have to quote the County regulations.'
'Headmasters and caretakers need educating.'
'Caretakers are often either bloody-minded or too old to want to do evening work.'

The effect of these difficulties on the way the role is performed, and in terms of the frustrations produced, is reflected in the observation that 'In the main we are using other people's premises and equipment; this leads to all sorts of petty things which take up time both in solving and trying to placate people.'

Within the College of Further Education where adult education does not have departmental status (FE. 2) there are more accommodation problems than where there is a department. In the questionnaire 60 per cent of respondents in the former category identified particular difficulties of sharing and status: 'Adult education is last in the priority list'; 'One begs often'; 'Adult education is peripheral'. They often referred specifically to the problems being 'insoluble at my level' and of being 'removed from policy making'. Difficulties of sharing were identified by 75 per cent of interviewees in Category FE. 2 and many observations pointed specifically to the consequences of a lack of status:

'I do not attend heads of department meetings and decisions are just handed down.'
'I'm not always aware of what other departments are doing.'
'I compete with departmental budgets and a head of department can veto a class; if they're worried about points or have underemployed teachers they're keen.'
'I've got to use full-timers but sometimes the people who are available for adult education work are not necessarily adult education people, but I have to use them because they're under hours.'
'Sometimes I have to include what a head of department wants in a programme to get what I want.'
'Adult education tends to lose its identity.'

Understandably tutors often feel that, 'If adult education was a department within the College it would have a better chance to compete with other priorities.' However, though the problems are not as frequently referred to where adult education has departmental status they are nevertheless still very important. Occasionally the comments are of the 'We are competing for accommodation' kind. Others suggest that 'adult education tends to get lost in the general working of the College'. More importantly, there is sometimes an awareness for heads of department of problems at a different level within the organisation – the academic board. The response here is by no means consistent, some clearly have difficulty, others just do not mention it. As academic boards are 'dominated by full-time 16–19 teachers' it is probable that 'I have lost before I start, they only pay lip service to adult education'. Or, as one battle-scarred adult educator put it:

'I think this is what will kill adult education in the Further Education College, the academic boards. They're the second biggest problem, I think. The first one is the County which is just insensitive to the effects of fee structures. But . . . I think in the long term we will look back upon academic boards as being ways of blowing your nose at the local population, because academic boards are interested in vocational and mainly full-time courses.'

In so far as the academic board is an arena in which departments compete for resources and where decisions are taken about their allocation, then it is not surprising that an adult educator has 'to put up very strong arguments to justify (his) part-time teachers' budget'. Access to a sympathetic principal, who reserves final decisions about resource allocation to himself, would appear to be a stronger position for adult education; indeed several principals indicated that they played a positive role in defending adult education within the college:

'I'm certainly not having any nonsense about adult education being less important.'
'I determined that adult education should not be neglected; in other colleges it is often the runt of the litter.'
'Adult education has parity with other departments.'
'We've protected the adult education budget.'

Are some of the difficulties of borrowing school accommodation, identified by both Specialised Institution principals and by College of Further Education organisers, mitigated by absorbing the adult education provision within a Community School? The evidence suggests that, if anything, they are heightened because of the daily work contact with the staff of the school; what in theory might be an advantage, that is regular contact, may turn out to be a marked disadvantage where school staff are unsympathetic to the work for adults. As in the College of Further Education the lack of standing of adult education produces important problems of identity and access to accommodation. There are undoubtedly many problems related to the need to compete with the major user, the school, with important consequences for the confidence of adult educators. In the interviews 74 per cent mentioned such difficulties and in both these and the questionnaire the problem of conflict over accommodation was often identified:

'If there is a clash of interest then we haven't got a snowball's chance in hell. Conflicts are reconciled in the interests of the school and there is very little day use.'
'There are clashes with school requirements in the evening and we often have to cancel a class.'
'There are conflicts over daytime use – it's bribery and corruption really – we're trying to move the school out of community use rooms.'

The last comment highlights a particular problem – where there is identifiable 'community use' accommodation the school, pressed for accommodation for its statutory work, has usually taken this over during the daytime; as one interviewee remarked, 'There is a difference between theory and practice'. In the use of space generally the impression gained is that there 'is a tendency for the community side to do most of the giving'. An important consequence is that there are surprisingly few daytime activities for adults in the programmes of Community Schools (see Table 7.1, column 4). There is a marked contrast here with both Colleges of Further Education and Specialised Institutions. The difference between Community Schools and Colleges of Further Education may be pointing to differences in the nature of the institutions – in general the latter are more likely to respond to difficulties about daytime accommodation within the institution by going to outside locations, such as church or village halls.

Headmasters are usually aware of these accommodation problems but see the use of community rooms by the school as an inevitable consequence of the size and growth of the school population. There were many references to the difficulties:

'There are in-built conflicts.'
'There are inevitable problems of trying to operate a number of different services from one building using one set of facilities.'
'Adult education has to fight its way through.'
'The school acquires nothing very tangible; our sewing machines are used by adults and we've engineered this now so that our dressmaking class is taught by our needlecraft teacher, which helps; our typewriters are pounded cheerfully through most nights by adults.'
'I can only give community education the secretarial time that it needs if I steal it from the secretaries that are here because we are a school. And so the students at school are suffering. It's exactly the same in terms of the tremendous use that we make of the equipment. We don't get the machinery replaced any more quickly in the design workshops because it's used twice a day instead of once. But in the end it's the students at school who suffer because it's their equipment and we are here primarily for their compulsory education. As I see it they are not getting such a first-rate deal as a result of this tremendous use.'

The last two quotations are an unusually specific acknowledgment of the frequent tendency for principals of Community Schools to identify not with the total institution but with the school.

As in a College of Further Education sharing problems are often compounded by the attitude of other staff in the organisation to the adult work. At best there might be 'a high degree of tolerance but no really shared concern'; at worst an 'antagonistic school staff who are jealous of the use of facilities – there is a constant calming down of day school staff and we are in a sense obliged to offer a class to an existing daytime teacher'. Or, more despairingly: 'There's an extent of hostility, if you like, against what you're trying to do even from the major institution you're working with. So you have to keep asking yourself why you are keeping on. My predecessor kept on for one year and then gave up . . . you have to really believe in continuing education to keep on doing it.' Other observations were that 'the staff see our work as subordinate'; 'they don't value it as being worthwhile', (or, more cheerfully, 'We get along . . . and generally we have a high degree of co-operation from the school staff'). The reaction of the authority to the need to economise may reinforce this attitude for when they cut the budget 'it reaffirms in people's minds, oh, it's not really worthwhile, it's just something round the edge'.

One consequence of this feeling of vulnerability, of being 'round the edge', is that community staff sometimes take on school duties over and above any formal expectation in their contract, as examinations or lettings officer, as fire officer or licensee; they like to be seen as having a role related to the whole school. Others use school teaching, either contractual or voluntary, as a means of establishing themselves:

'Teaching A level helps tremendously your standing with school staff. 'The essential thing for community development is my relation with the daytime staff. If I were a full-time youth leader or a full-time adult man I wouldn't be accepted in the staff room as I obviously am at the moment . . . they feel they can come to me and moan and as a school teacher I will be on their side.'

Additionally, a teaching role may be welcomed as a way of keeping the options open in career development terms. Sometimes headmasters will encourage involvement in the school because they recognise the problem: 'I doubted whether the staff knew what the Community people were doing, therefore I integrated them right into the school.' One head had deliberately appointed people with experience of teaching in the school 'because of the considerable hostility to the community school set-up'. Other heads recognised aspects of the problem but could not see what could be done:

'The adult educator and the school staff have different life styles; time appears much less important in adult education, it's more leisurely.' 'It's a fairly isolated role; they work mainly at night and have little interrelationship with the "day-shift".' 'Our school staff haven't got it into their bones.'

Any role tension which community staff may feel as a result of their relatively low standing in the school is likely to be exacerbated by the often inadequate definition of the role by their employers. Comments like 'There isn't any coherent idea about the role', or 'We are trying very hard to define precisely what community education is', or 'It may be that the aim we are given of integrating with the school is an impossible one' identify the doubts which are frequently felt. Roughly one in three headmasters indicated an awareness of this role tension:

'We are inventing it as we go along.'

'Nobody has any idea what Community School means.'
'The language is a real problem and shows the extent of our own confusion.'
'The Community School or College seems to me at the moment to have such barriers of bad thinking in it that it's not going to get terribly far.'

The doubts which heads sometimes have about the concept clearly are visited on the community staff; not all share these doubts but among those that do the result may well be, as one adult educator claimed, 'I have never felt other than alienated.'

Reference was made earlier to the role of sympathetic principals in Colleges of Further Education who defend adult education within the College. Do Community School headmasters adopt the same role? It would seem not for they tend to see their job in relation to the adult side of community work rather more passively as 'listeners' or 'counsellors'. Some identified the 'arbitrator' role; as one head observed, 'Someone's got to blow the whistle when there's a conflict over the use of facilities.' In general, heads of Community Schools appear to spend less time on the adult side of their job than do principals of Colleges of Further Education. Although most acknowledged it was a difficult calculation to make, only 30 per cent of the principals of Colleges of Further Education failed to identify the percentage of their time devoted to adult education (average 15 per cent). In contrast over two-thirds of heads of Community Schools were unable to identify any specific time commitment and typical responses were as follows:

'Not so much time as I would like; the problems that come up are problems within the statutory age group.'
'I have a tenuous contact.'
'I have no grass roots contact with adult education, I have a large management job to do.'
'I delegate – have only been in a couple of times to adult education activities.'
'The school takes up most of my time.'
'I often feel my involvement is nominal and limited. I try to suggest that I'm interested in what the adults do. . . .'

It is very probable, therefore, that heads of Community Schools are much less involved in the adult aspects of the work than their counterparts in Colleges of Further Education; exceptions are to be found but the proposition remains intact. Additionally, where adult education has departmental status principals of Colleges of Further Education also adopt a supportive role outside of the college:

'I feel it appropriate that I do battle on behalf of AE and bring the strength of the Principal to bear rather than them having to challenge on their own.'
'I can play a stronger line as the Principal of a major institution, particularly with the aid of my governing body, than they could do running solo and reporting direct to County Hall.'

'I must be seen as the flag bearer of the adult education cause.'
'I defend the status and significance of AE wherever I can, at County Hall, in the Governors, in the press.'

The motives behind the adoption of this political role are apparently a mixture of commitment to adult education and, probably more important, the interests of the college. It is significant that all of the above quotations are taken from interviews in colleges where there was a department of adult education. Therefore any personal commitment was likely to be strongly reinforced by a desire to protect an important, and often large, aspect of the institution's work. Indeed one principal freely acknowledged that his motive was essentially an institutional one; 'I encourage the development of AE in order to maintain the viability of the institution'; adult education can be an important determinant of a college's grading. These observations lend support to the view expressed in the Russell Report (para. 356) that if adult education is to be based in a College of Further Education it should have departmental status.

The external political role identified by College of Further Education principals was not referred to by Community School headmasters. The general tendency for adult education to be more protected in the former environment is likely to be further strengthened by budgetary arrangements. In a College of Further Education the service competes for its resources within a total college budget; in Community Schools it is separately financed and is, therefore, more vulnerable to externally generated pressures for economy. Within a college, spending on adult education can be 'hidden' in total institutional expenditure and as a result can be protected by a sympathetic principal. As a senior officer observed:

'One of the ways we've been able to protect adult education over the years has been by the very fact that locating it within the colleges and within college budgets it's not been a separate item that can be easily attacked and it's been protected within the umbrella of further education. I know that has its dangers – you can have a principal who is antagonistic and is prepared to put all his resources say into engineering or something else – but as the people with the chief responsibility have the status of heads of departments they are able to exercise considerable authority.'

We have tended so far to concentrate on the negative factors inherent for adult education staff within a multi-purpose institution, we have been concerned, that is, with job dissatisfaction. However, in both Colleges of Further Education and Community Schools adult educators were agreed on certain basic advantages of their situation by comparison with Specialised Institutions; these advantages were identified mainly in terms of facilities and staffing. Sometimes College of Further Education interviewees referred, for example, to the 'whole college around us – we can interchange staff and ideas and we have the accommodation'; more frequently, in both Colleges of Further Education and Community Schools, reference was made to the limitations of the Specialised Institution in terms of its lack of resources or its isolation. However, staff in Community Schools almost invariably saw their situation as preferable to a College of Further Education and vice versa. In the former situation the College of Further Education was sometimes regarded as 'the worst sort of environment', or as 'having other priorities' and 'fewer community links'. Similar criticism of Colleges of Further Education was expressed by principals of Specialised Institutions with experience of working in such organisations:

'I would never want to go back, I found it very stultifying and we were really bottom of the pile.'

'The important thing for us is people not the system.'

'In the College of Further Education we had the expertise, the facilities and the range of courses but student lacked identity in the social sense.'

For their part College of Further Education staff were often very critical of Community Schools. Their observations related mainly to problems of built-in conflict, the prior claim of school pupils and the attitude of the headmaster. One person with experience of working in a Community School had 'reservations about applying the concept to the benefit of the adult population because it is constrained to serve young people first'. Others were convinced that Community Schools were 'plagued with problems of conflict'. Principals of Specialised Institutions were even more critical of the Community School, over half being strongly opposed to the concept. One, with Community School experience, pointed to the lack of daytime activities for adults, and another, who had spent five years as an adult tutor in a Community School, summed up the views of many of his colleagues who had not had direct experience:

'The Community College is a fantastic idea but its great deficiency is that the head of the College is also head of the School and he or she is chosen as a result of their school experience and the pecking order is definitely school first and they don't relate to adults very much. I think there is definitely another great deficiency – the whole thing about adult education is that the professional never talks down to the student, you are equals, but if you've had a successful career on the school side you tend to be authoritarian.'

Another criticism levelled by Specialised Institute principals at multipurpose institutions in general was that they were 'too large' and in consequence 'too impersonal' or 'formalised'. The typical view was that a large institution was 'off-putting' to students and as one person observed, 'Though I have the confidence to ask my way about I don't know how long students would persevere before their nerve gave out'. Though College of Further Education staff seemed unaware of this problem Community School staff sometimes were: 'The building is challenging, horrifying to the local community'; 'People don't realise how hard it is for adults to come into the school.'

Aspects of role conflict

It was to be expected that a joint (i.e. part-time) college or school teaching/adult education appointment would produce elements of role conflict. There were, however, mixed views on this. Only occasionally were there references to its being 'only possible to do the adult education job properly', or that the adult work was 'plenty for one person to do'. There were also some references to the difficulty of containing such a diffuse task as adult education:

'They've got me on two mornings and one afternoon, a sort of three session thing, which I'm not happy with. I don't think it's fair to the children. . . . I won't say it's not fair to me, but I don't really give my mind fully to the school teaching job; it's such a small proportion of the time that if somebody has just rung up with a problem you tend to carry that problem in and be thinking about it when you ought to be dealing with those poor children.'

One College of Further Education interviewee pointed to the particular difficulty of trying to tackle teacher supervision: 'With the part-time teachers I'm the boss as it were but with the full-time College staff I'm just another lecturer with a particular responsibility . . . this is where I find most antagonism to my presence.' But such comments were exceptional and many expressed a preference for a combined teaching/adult education role, partly on the grounds that it 'keeps your hand in' but also because it gives the individual some standing within the college; this reaction would be consistent with the already noted response of some Community School staff. However, other Community School tutors do find the joint role very demanding, particularly where it is a contractual requirement, and would prefer to concentrate only on the adult side. Such a reaction would not be surprising in situations in which, as one Community School principal remarked, 'You can't mould the whole timetable around them, so therefore they just don't fit in.'

'Well at the moment I spend four periods with this Humanities Department, I spend four or five periods supervising in the library, I have one period on handwriting and one is an English period.

English is your specialism, is it?

No, Religious Education is my specialism. At least it was.'

In consequence some Community School tutors are 'not happy' with the particular teaching they are asked to do.

There is evidence of another important aspect of role conflict. In all types of institution there is a strong possibility that the adult educator will find that his work interferes with his home life. This is partly due to the number of hours worked but more importantly to their unsocial nature, indeed adult educators are sometimes seen by their colleagues as the 'night shift'. A fourteen or fifteen session week, much of it in the evenings and weekends, is not uncommon and the consequences are reflected in the following:

'It makes you very tired.'
'People wear themselves out very quickly in adult education.'
'My family suffers, the work excludes almost everything else.'
'I find this job affects your family life, it's so all-consuming.'
'I have difficulty keeping my wife happy with all the hours away.'
'It is essential to have a stable home background for this job, otherwise you couldn't survive.'
'My marriage has suffered enormously over the years that I have been in adult education, and not just my marriage but the children have suffered and been deprived of time and attention just as my wife has. . . . There is a tendency for people in adult education to be intense about their work . . . even if they only worked ten sessions a week on the premises they would be taking work home in their heads, mulling it over and worrying about it. In fact of course they don't work ten sessions. . . . I have averaged fourteen sessions a week; I'm sure of it.'
'One of the things I have to do constantly is try to look after the health of the full-time staff because they will work all the time.'

In some Community Schools principals are very much aware of the tendency to overwork:

'They have too much work and not enough support.'
'Their job just gets bigger and bigger.'
'They are idealistic and tend to be generous with their time and can work themselves to death.'

In authorities with a specialised, full-time service it is the officer at County Hall who is likely to express similar views:

'Independent principals identify with an adult education movement. All our principals live, eat and sleep adult education almost to a fault, we wish they'd relax now and again. We just can't complain that we're not getting value for money.'
'Principals feel that if they're sitting at home on a weekday evening they're not doing their job.'

Nor is it only full-time adult educators who overwork:

'It is meant to be a part-time job but I have found that it is nearly a full-time job. . . . It's a fairly full day, and then I take work home in the evening.'
'I am employed for three evenings a week which, having built up the centre as I have, is plain silly; you can't do it. I put in five nights a week plus at least two afternoons.'

Not infrequently the work will intrude directly into the home with the adult educator's wife becoming a clerical assistant/telephonist, usually unpaid.

There seems no doubt that all kinds and all grades of adult educators are prone to overwork themselves and that, though some employers seek to protect them from this tendency more are inclined to ignore it. This general failure to give adult educators sufficient clerical and other support obviously reduces the efficiency and enterprise of their educational work, but it also affects their personal and family life.

Summary and conclusions

In summary, it is possible to identify several contrasts and similarities in the job satisfactions of staff working in different types of institution. In terms of career prospects the principal of a Specialised Institution does not seem to be as well placed as staff in multi-purpose institutions, where the options are still open in that there is the possibility of pursuing a career either in adult or an alternative field of education. However, whatever career disadvantages may exist for the principal of a Specialised Institution they are more than compensated for by the autonomy of his appointment; he is very much his own boss. In contrast, in multi-purpose institutions there is much less freedom of action.

Adult educators in each type of institution identify the lack of finance as an important job constraint; however, it is most keenly felt where there are large programmes in Specialised Institutions and Colleges of Further Education. This is likely to be experienced as a source of frustration – the adult educator has an idea of how the job might be better done but lacks the resources to realise this. There are other very marked areas of role tension and probable conflict. Within the job there is often a clash between the administrative and educational aspects of the work, though this is much more keenly felt in Specialised Institutions than elsewhere. Additionally, there is a strong possibility of conflict between the demands of the job and family commitments.

There are many problems in the use of school or college premises which are certainly no less acute in Community Schools. It can be concluded that the hopes of the Russell Report have not been achieved in many authorities; teachers often still 'claim exclusive rights to publicly provided equipment' and many head teachers still 'protect the school building from being used as an adult institute'. The hoped for 'spirit of co-operation' is frequently not to be found and the difficulties are likely to prove insurmountable unless local authorities provide 'adequate caretaking and cleaning services' and allow for 'faster depreciation' of plant and equipment (paras. 318, 343). The present difficulties of sharing and of attitudes to adult education in multi-purpose institutions must raise serious doubts about their stated advantages both in terms of the resources available and of their effective use.

If further evidence is needed about the difficulties of adult educators operating in borrowed school premises it can be gleaned from the interviews with spare-time staff working in a specialised service. In one sense their experience relates to that of Community School or College of Further Education staff, for although they work in a separate and specialised service they are, nevertheless, very frequently employed in the school in which they run their 'evening centre'. Many clearly feel the conflict built in to such an arrangement, of knowing where their 'loyalties lie'; others have solved the problem by working as an evening centre head in another school altogether. However, whether in their own or another school, most identify the difficulties of borrowing accommodation in the same terms as their colleagues in other kinds of institution; (among those that do not are to be found headmasters who operate as evening centre heads and must be tempted to keep evening provision down to a level which causes least disturbance to school activities).

'School demands in the evenings create rather a lot of problems.'
'I accept what the head will kindly give me.'
'It's a matter of great delicacy and diplomacy – of biting your tongue and grinning and bearing it.'
'The head is happy if we use one of his staff.'
'I wanted to offer pottery but the day-school staff were uncooperative . . . none of them would take it so it had to be dropped.'

Clearly, as in other situations, school staff frequently behave as if they have 'a divine right to the accommodation and equipment'; the same spare-time principal concluded that, 'If I want something I have to beg.'

Local authority policy on dual use, though evidence of goodwill, is often relatively ineffective. The associated difficulties were commented on earlier; it is clearly not enough to say what should happen in situations in which adult educators borrow premises, the problem still remains of making the arrangements work in the face of the often conflicting needs of the school and its staff. Senior officers are often aware of the problem:

'And is there anything laid down which encourages them to use school premises for adult education or is it entirely at their discretion?
This is largely at the discretion of the school head, dare I say largely at the discretion of the school caretaker in many instances because although I've not mentioned this particular gentleman before it is the school caretaker I think who probably has a greater influence on adult education in this Authority than any other class of county council employee. The articles of government for all secondary schools require the governors of those secondary schools to have due regard to the county council's policy of dual use, which, broadly speaking, says that dual use shall happen but doesn't really say how it shall happen.'

It can only be concluded that little seems to have changed since Russell; adult education is still too often the unwelcome borrower of other people's premises or alternatively the unequal partner in a sharing situation.

References

1. **Nolte, C. M.** (ed.), (1966) *An Introduction to School Administration: Selected Readings*, New York, p. 259.
2. **Burnham, P. S.** (1969), in Baron, G. and Taylor, W. (eds.), *Educational Administration and the Social Sciences*, London, p. 90.
3. **Clark, Burton R.** (1956) *The Marginality of Adult Education*, Boston, p. 1.

Chapter 9

Adult educators: attitudes and issues

Adult educators are typically eager to talk about the philosophical framework within which they approach their work; in the interviews different values and attitudes emerged as did wide ranging views on relevant concepts and issues. These views are presented here. Our purpose has been to let the practitioners speak for themselves, limiting comment to the need to link their observations and to relate these where appropriate to their situation and to practice in different kinds of institution.

Community

It is not only Community School practitioners who see themselves as being in community education; adult educators in all types of institution see it as being part of their function, even if they have difficulty in defining it. The concept is protean of course but it usually implies an attempt to reach out to new sectors of the population and to discover needs which adult education can be instrumental in meeting in, for example, an immigrant community, an area of urban redevelopment, a day centre for the mentally handicapped or a home for the elderly. The essential aspect is that the adult educator is drawn out of his centre and gets involved in the community:

'The adult education centre is a place where someone can be contacted who will go out into the community . . . the right way is for A.E. to go outwards.'

'That's a dimension of a community service, that the people involved in it get drawn outside their institutions, however wide their institutions are; and they get drawn into that because of the kind of activity they get involved in. I mean if they were just concerned with setting up archaeology classes they might be able to contain themselves, but once you start talking about English for Immigrants, once you start talking about a literacy scheme in an area like that, you can see how you're going to get involved.'

It is often identified as a breaking down of traditional boundaries, as a move away 'from the education scene towards social therapy and community development'. Again,

The whole thing is much wider, we're emphasising now that you're reaching out into the community, doing community development of an educational nature and that's very, very difficult: but we've got to affect people's daily lives almost. It isn't enough just to amuse them and paper over the cracks of their needs as it were for one night per week or one afternoon or whatever it may be; you've got to have some impact on their daily living and reach out to them, not just by providing a disadvantaged group exercise, . . . but in some way we've got to help them within their communities.'

Though generally the concept evokes enthusiasm some have doubts about their own function and role:

'Job identification – exactly where are you going in a changing professional world and what are your priorities? How relevant are your particular skills, your experience and qualifications to this changing job? I remember some years ago the old lads as it were saying to me we're not social workers, and we had many debates about what was social work and what was education. My attitude on this is no we're not social workers but as educationalists we're helping people, in many ways – obviously there's a whole spectrum here of academic education, widening horizons, etc.'

There are also doubts of a more general kind:

'How can you talk of community when you only reach 5 per cent or 10 per cent of them anyway?'
'I'm not sure that local communities would want to be integrated even if they could be.'

Both the enthusiasm for and the doubts about a community role seem to reflect the general feeling of insecurity which many adult educators share. On the one hand *Community* is a concept which often has wide support outside of the service – it gives to the adult educator the social approval which he feels he often lacks; on the other, doubts about the role may exacerbate his existing insecurity. Such feelings would be damaging to any occupational group; they are doubly so to one whose members are as wholly committed to their work as are most full-time adult educators. Their superiors in Local Education Authorities sometimes find this need for a measure of approval and security difficult to cope with: 'I think they feel that their reason for being isn't fully accepted. . . . Sometimes they have the same doubts themselves, it isn't just that they see it in other people's eyes.' The less sympathetic describe them as 'a bit neurotic, always wanting reassurance'.

Far from being neurotic, the anxieties of adult educators seem to us to be sensible and justified. They have real causes, which need only to be listed:
(a) They are facing cutbacks proportionately more severe than those imposed upon any other part of the education service.
(b) They are still frequently regarded as providing 'mere' recreation

which does not merit public funding: the assumption is, presumably that 'real' education cannot be enjoyed: it must be nasty (like 'real' medicine), examined and preferably job-related.

(c) Their work is subject to the iron law of educational demand: the more education a man has the more likely he is to want more and the better able he is to get it. So their clients tend to be middle and lower middle rather than working class.

In this situation it is entirely natural that full-time adult educators should feel predisposed towards concepts of adult education and fields of work which seem likely to have an instrumental value and to give them the social approval which they need. So the *Community* concept is often given a strong emotional loading.

Compensation

The above comments seem to be even more relevant to the *Compensation* concept. Work for the disadvantaged invokes humanitarian and egalitarian values which have long been implicit in adult education, offers an alternative to the 'middle-class' image, and gains instant social approval and support. So it is not surprising that it is sometimes spoken of not just as a valuable field of work, but as 'a lifeline', or that normal provision is often sacrificed to it. Its political value is obvious:

'We've been able to talk about literacy, we've been able to talk about this expansion in the down-town areas, we've been able to talk about mentally handicapped, we've been able to talk about retired and retiring people; what we've done is to keep a trickle of reports going to committee about indisputable areas of community concern. People say what do you do about all this argument about flower arranging and so on: I say I don't have it these days. Where I used to try to argue, to justify, flower arranging, ballroom dancing and so on I don't do it now, I turn the conversation to talk about English for Asian Ladies or Literacy. The committee would rather talk about that than be embarrassed by trying to justify flower arrangement. I think in the F.E. sub-Committees I can't remember one of the usual disparaging remarks. You know them, about badminton and so on.'

Others, whilst recognising the instrumental value of compensatory work, have doubts about the consequences: ' We may be going too far along the disadvantage road and getting it out of balance but they're a group that, emotionally if you like, ring the bells with the people who hold the purse strings and we need to be alive to that.' In the present economic climate expansion of a compensatory programme is usually financed by cutting traditional areas of the programme and many adult educators are concerned about this diversion of resources. We shall have occasion to develop this theme further in looking at the current difficulties in the service (Ch. 10).

Recreation

The *Recreation* function of adult education, often felt to be its Achilles' heel, can be defended by linking it with *Compensation*; in this way it is presented as having an important social and therapeutic value:

*'There's a real social thing here and it seems to me very often, that the evening they spend here, whether it's knocking their brains out against the tutor in a Sociology class or in fact keeping fit or painting or what have you, might make the difference between that person retaining a balance, an equilibrium of some sort, and literally going to the doctor because they're depressed. I really see that as a real thing and I've seen the release and the relief on people's faces when they can get out for the evening; particularly women, because it seems to me they've been terribly constrained and still are in our society; and when they do get in here it's great to see, its their thing – and that's terribly important, isn't it. So I think it has a tremendous therapeutic value and a very great social value, apart from anything related vaguely to the term education'.
'I really do think that we make a serious contribution to the psychiatric welfare of a large number of people who are on the borderline; we give them somewhere to come, someone to talk to, something to do, and something to help them make themselves people.'*

What is usually thought of as simply recreation can be regarded as truly educational if education is equated with learning: 'Education means you learn something, and you can learn an awful lot by sitting over a cribbage table and talking to your friends . . . and I feel that this is an area that we're not in touch with.' It is an odd concept of education, but it seems democratic, not elitist and not middle class, and so may evoke similar feelings of social approval as do *Community* and *Compensatory* education:

'However effective and efficient our organisation may be within an L.E.A. or a University Department or a W.E.A. district, we're touching such a tiny minority of the population that we are at risk of suggesting that over 90 per cent of the population, the adult population is not learning. In reality if we recognise what is happening in social grouping in pubs and clubs and at work, in churches and the football ground and all the rest of it, there is a very real community learning experience that we must recognise.'

So if *Participation* is held to have a social and educational value in itself *Recreation* is given the social approval which it would otherwise lack.

Participation

This concept has more than one connotation. The adult educator may simply wish to get non-users involved but on their terms: 'The first time we run the class we don't intervene, we like it just to occur, and then afterwards we begin to intervene. We say if you want to run a class on climbing trees then we'll deal with it after you've started, because very often of course we find that if we say "no" they never come again.'

Such an approach may have strong overtones of *Community*; here for example is an adult educator speaking about a community education project:

'I sent out a letter to various selected people, and they were selected because they weren't involved in anything, I deliberately avoided people who would be the leaders of the community like the vicar and the heads of the schools and the local councillors and people like this, people who would dominate a gathering; but rather invited people who went to the working men's club and said bring along your wife, tell your mates, and so on. I was rather pleased because about fifty people turned up at this gathering. We sat around and we had a few drinks and we got to talking about what was happening in the village, or what wasn't, and they were all very ready to say what there wasn't. I think that was probably, since it was the first time it had happened, the best experience I've ever had in the time I've had in adult education, it was a fantastic experience. I felt that if the whole thing had ended then something had been achieved, that those people left that room and in some way they were different.

There is no mistaking the missionary zeal and the strength of feeling involved. And there is a similar zest in the unpredictable consequences of a situation in which it is the community groups, not the adult educator, which 'call the tune' – in spite of the wry comment at the end:

'The more you expose yourself to this community, wherever you are, the thing takes on. There are some people who can still preserve nice quiet neatly-run adult education centres and it's a joy to visit, very comforting, to motor up in your motor-car, find a dozen classes neatly run, neatly planned – all that I used to do twenty years ago myself – calling the tune, very comforting. But that mass of activities you get down town in the evening; it's out of control – well not out of control but beyond the resources.'

Another aspect of *Participation*, of adults determining their own activities, is their involvement in the management of centres: 85 per cent of the Community Schools and 70 per cent of Specialised Institutes (Sp.1 and 2) had some formal student participation through an 'association', a 'council' or a 'committee'. [In Colleges of Further Education these arrangements are rarely to be found.] In commenting on the part students played 'in running the centre' few outside of Community Schools identified areas of involvement other than fund raising or organising the social side of the centre; programme planning is only exceptionally an activity which closely engages students. Even in some Community Schools we were told that 'they ratify my decision', and 'in most cases, let's be honest, they leave it to me'. Again, 'they don't meet very often and I take the day-to-day decisions – decision-making power rests with me'. Sometimes the headmaster plays a significant role: 'I think the Head is very skilful, he can guide them really as he thinks fit.' Exceptionally 'they plan the programme'.

In Specialised Institutions student participation is mainly in fund raising and social activities; in the area of programme planning, 'I pick the ideas from students' or 'I decide the programme' is much more typical than 'they have a real say'. In general, therefore, the relationship appears to be of the 'I keep them informed', 'They advise where they can' kind. However, a few interviewees did see an emerging role for student committees in the context of economic pressures on the service, a kind of political activity in bringing pressure to bear on the local authority. Indeed one Specialised Institute practitioner had set up his students' committee because he needed such support and another had encouraged his committee 'to think that they have some executive authority because the only way forward it seems to me for adult education is to get the local situation sufficiently strong to hammer loud and hard enough on the door to command a return'. A similar point was made in a Community School where the committee had 'been militant in the face of fee increases'.

Despite the philosophy of participation which underlies the Community School concept, and the activities of the Educational Centres Association, there is sometimes a basic mistrust of the whole idea by adult educators; their concern in this area has already been examined (Ch. 7). It is sufficient to note here that unfavourable attitudes to student participation in programme planning were voiced more frequently than were any expressions of commitment.

Continuing education

The concept of lifelong continuing education is built into the philosophy and the structure of the Community School and exerts a strong institutional pressure upon members of staff. Headmasters in such institutions readily identify the beneficial consequences resulting from having both adults and children in the same organisation:

'There are I think a great many reasons why an institution of this kind should include adult education during the day. One of the major reasons is that youngsters in the school, 11–16, who had they gone to a normal school would have been given the impression, as I think most people are, that somehow or other when you're being educated you're taken out of the community and you're isolated in a building called a school until you're educated and civilised sufficiently to be allowed back into the community again, and that education doesn't really have anything to do with the community or real life and by association the teachers have very little to offer in connection with your life. Now the youngsters who come here can't get that impression, they can see the library and the sports centre being used throughout the day by adults as

well as themselves, they can see adults being educated, all our dining areas are being used by adults and members of the community at the same time as they're being used by students and staff, and really they must begin to realise that education is part of total community living and also that education is part of an on-going process through life.'

'I would like to see the school building up a continuum into adult education where once they left school people continued with leisure and other activities associated with the adult aspect of the centre.'

'I'm for continuance in education, that's why I prefer the community school with its sixth form because it's a fairly natural way of growing up.'

Adult educators in Community Schools make the same points by reference to 'education for life', or to the fact that 'pupils can easily make the transition'.

An interesting aspect of these quotaions is that they tend to focus on benefits to the school and to its pupils rather than to adults. Indeed Community School headmasters stress the benefits to the school more frequently than they do the idea of continuing education as such, largely in terms of the effect which adults have on the standards of behaviour among pupils:

'The advantages of the Community School are that we do get parents and children coming to the same place. I don't know whether this is beneficial to the adults but it's enormously beneficial to the school.'

'The Community School is a good economic thing with side benefits for adult students. Adults set behaviour standards for the school and at the same time gain some insight into children and schools.'

'We see the value of adults coming into sixth form classes as setting higher standards of behaviour for our sixth formers.'

'It helps the class behave in a different sort of way with adults around so we don't get the disciplinary problems that one reads about. It encourages the youngsters if they can see Mrs. Brown is slogging through homework and handing it in on time and is really keen.'

'I'm interested in educating children first – I do emphasise that my interest in the Community School has a sort of key in this factor of importance of the contacts between the school and the community as far as real educational gain for young people is concerned . . . that's the key factor in my motivation and I wouldn't want to hide that. I believe that our ability to educate young people is greatly helped by the attitude of its own community to the school and I think that in turn is greatly helped the more open the school is rather than the more closed the school is.'

The starting point is therefore the pupil and the interests of the school; the benefits for adults are less certain. Indeed the only explicit benefits are that they 'gain some insight into children and schools', and have access to school classes. The latter is an oft-quoted benefit of a Community School and yet in practice the adult in a school class is still the exception. Less than half of headmasters indicated that it was happening and of these most had only one or two adult students in classes, mainly for O and A level:

'We have very few adults.'
'Last year we had one parent in A level.'
'We do admit a few to sixth form work.'

There was only one exception to this picture – in one school there were some thirty adults in examination classes. Evening classes are sometimes used in order to widen the subject range for school pupils, often in languages where it is possible to run, say, Russian by mixing pupils and adults; the latter also gain from such an arrangement, though this may be incidental.

The difficulties which adults are frequently likely to face in trying to join school classes are reflected in the following quotes from interviews with Community School headmasters:

'It is a rare housewife who can fit in with our particular timetable.'
'It's a gesture of goodwill on the part of our staff.'
'I told the adults that I reserved the right to ask them to leave if it didn't work out.'

It appears, therefore, that the adult is generally there on sufferance – come in if the times suit but don't make difficulties for the staff. There are, no doubt, rare exceptions to be found but the overall impression is very strong. In contrast, in Colleges of Further Education, there is a much greater willingness to accommodate adults not only in O and A level courses but also by providing role education for such groups as playgroup leaders, home helps and the Samaritans. Several had also pioneered 'return to learning' course for adults. These activities reflect the desire to break down the barriers between the vocational and non-vocational aspects of the work. One adult educator operating in a College of Further Education, who had spent several years in a Community Schools, expressed the contrast between the two situations as he saw them as follows:

'I think that we will move away in Adult Education from the present emphasis on community towards a much broader concept of educational opportunities throughout life with no distinction between what is vocational and what isn't. For some, if we get paid educational leave, that might be on a more substantial and organized basis than a two hour a week class; that won't ever really give the kind of flesh to Adult Education that it needs unless we can convince the public at large, the government in particular, that individuals have educational needs that do not terminate when their educational apprenticeship for life is served, you know by the age of 16 or 18 or whatever it might be, but I think that is what one will be moving towards. I think we're well placed in terms of general daytime activities for full-time and second chance opportunities for women – I think that is important. We are able to offer

a range of O level and A level courses which give meaning to the notion of a broad curriculum of activities for the adult population which isn't possible in a school setting although you are finding that room is being found for individual adults to go along to school classes.'

It is, of course, not only in multi-purpose institutions that the idea of continuing education is current. In Specialised Institutions, also, adult educators seek to break down the barriers between age-groups and between vocational and non-vocational education:

'It's not necessary to have these artificial administrative divisions, and we can create a much more sensible and a fuller educational service by working with people of all ages.'

'We have from five- to eighty-year-olds in one marvellous workshop.... I keep every door open so there's a terrific movement all the time: if they want to go into woodwork for a couple of weeks to start making a table base or something or other and then they want to go up to soft furnishing to make the lampshade to go on it – or mum does the lampshade while son does the base – they can do just this. Or if they all want to go in and make a sledge – father, mother and two children – they do just that; they work as a team on it.'

'In an area like this there are a lot of people who are educationally deprived and if you can get them along to a course which offers a qualification of some sort its amazing how much potential they reveal.'

Adult and youth

Continuing education also finds expression in the linking of adult education with youth work. On balance this is an aspect of continuity of which practitioners disapprove, whatever kind of service they may work in:

'Adults want a separate service and the two groups don't mix.' (AY)
'I don't believe a youth club has a place in a school complex.' (Comm.)
'I see youth groups as a threat to the ethos of a school, the informal contacts conflict with school needs.' (Comm.)
'I don't really believe, at field level, that youth in practice mixes with adult education. The youth club runs a disco and attempts to shake the building to pieces – adult students have commented that they don't feel happy in a noisy atmosphere.' (Sp.)
'Adults feel that they like to have something for themselves.' (Sp.)
'I think that children and adolescents want to do their thing and adults want to do their thing. If its a natural marriage I don't mind, but I don't want shotgun marriages.'(Sp.)
'I think on the whole youth service personnel are orientated towards the immature, if I may use that word, and I think we're orientated towards the mature; and I do think the things are very different. I think the whole basis of their work is informality and lack of structure, and I think in

education as such there must be some formality and some structure. There's no reason I suppose why a person shouldn't be trained to do both if he's the right animal, but whether there are that number of right animals about . . . .' (FE.)

On the other hand:

'Adult and youth are inseparable philosophically.'(AY)
'I'd love the youth in with adults, I think it's nonsense to cut them in two.'(Sp.)
'I'd rather have youth insulated not isolated; I like a separate building because I'm not faced with the problem of interference.' (Comm.)

The latter quotation summarises a compromise position acceptable to some practitioners in Community Schools; insulation rather than isolation. However, the balance of opinion in such institutions is still unfavourable. (Though, of course, the result would have been different had we talked to youth tutors.) Typically the rejection of the youth link is related, as in the case of adults in school classes, to behaviour standards – adults are welcome because they set appropriate standards, youth are best kept separate because they do not – they threaten 'the ethos of a school'.

A self-supporting service

Programme analysis has already shown that different kinds of institution have varying levels of commitment to *Compensatory* education. Such differences were likely to be reflected to some extent in the answers to the following interview question: 'It seems possible that non-vocational education may be forced to become financially self-supporting. If this were so, what long-term effect do you think it would have?' Approximately half of all those interviewed saw self-supporting arrangements as at worst a *disaster* or at best resulting in adult education becoming, unacceptably, even more a *middle class preserve.* The many quotations given below are an expression of the very great strength of feeling – on no other issue did adult educators take up such a strongly critical stance.

Specialised Institutions
'It would be goodbye adult education in my area . . . it would destroy me.'
'An elitist service for those who can afford to pay.'
'It would result in a private educational club made up of middle and upper classes – adult education for the chosen few.'
'It would wipe out most of the work I have developed – without special provision it would cut out work in the poorer areas.'
'The workers would become disenchanted. I can put up with my blue rinse ladies because I know we are doing nicely at X. We would end up promoting more for those that have.'

Colleges of Further Education
'We would have more and more people who have already benefited from education.'
'We'd lose the disadvantaged work – people like myself might as well not be here if society does not want this kind of service unless it pays for itself.'
'A bloody awful idea – once again education for the middle class.'
'Disastrous – authorities are using fee increases as a back door method of closing the service down.'

Adult/Youth
'I get depressed beyond belief at the thought – it would be tragic.'
'It would become a class service and it would not be giving, as was indeed intended, a second-chance education for the deprived and disadvantaged.'
'. . . the straw that broke the camel's back – I wouldn't have a programme.'

Community Schools
'It would fall apart. I think that any authority that's doing it is playing a con-trick. I think what they're saying is we don't want classes but we are not going to have it levelled against us that we stopped them . . . if we do it this way it will kill itself.'
'I might as well pack up and go home.'

There is no doubting the great strength of feeling which unites most adult educators on this issue; it would cripple work of a compensatory nature, it is a back door method of closing the service down. However, there was a marked difference in response in Community Schools (Comm. 1) where only one in four saw it as a disaster or as creating a middle class preserve. Though some Colleges of Further Education and Specialised Institute practitioners indicated that they would try to find other sources of funds and would use volunteer labour rather than see the service die, they clearly saw self-supporting arrangements as a serious threat to the kind of service they wanted to run. Indeed, several indicated they would not be prepared to work under such arrangements. In contrast many Community School interviewees did not see such arrangements as posing a threat to the kind of service they wanted to run:

'This is a middle class town. I accept that the middle class are also people and it doesn't worry me that A.E. appeals particularly to them. . . . I don't think we need feel guilty about it.'
'It should be nearer self-supporting, I think we are getting it at a ridiculously low price.'
'There are some things I wouldn't mind dropping – even without classes there would be a lot going on and people would become more involved in decision making.'

The last two quotations identify a concept of adult education concerned with *Participation*. Support for the contention that 'even without classes there would be a lot going on' can be found by reference to the number of clubs and societies affiliated to the typical Community School. Such affiliations, linking the *Participation* and the *Recreation* concepts of adult education, may encourage a favourable attitude to the idea of the service being self-supporting. It can now be seen not as a threat but as a healthy development, for if students run their own recreational activities the very fact of their doing so is felt to give those activities an educational value:

'It's forcing upon us something that I've been working towards and encouraging for all the time I've been in adult education, and that's the formation of self-programming groups.'
'We encourage the growth of clubs. It not only saves us, saves the Authority, money, it's good because they can budget for themselves and run their own thing.'

Teaching

Many adult educators assert the primacy of educational values – they express a belief that the enlargement of an individual's skill and understanding by skilled and sensitive teaching is a value in itself, irrespective of any other purposes it may achieve. Their response to cutbacks and economies may be a reassertion of such values and a concentration upon these rather than, for example, upon *Compensation* or *Participation*. This, as the following quotations suggest, provides its own kind of 'excitement' for both staff and students.

'Development is very much down into the course material and developing the course and widening it out, and getting your teachers, even if they are only doing two hours a week, to really look at their courses. With this no-growth in tutor hours this is the only way we can bring excitement into the work, I think you will agree with me you've got to move: these places can never stand still or else they die, and the excitement of these places are the new interests you can bring in. Now, if you can't grow, you've got to bring new interest somewhere, so the exercise now for us all is to bring a new width and breadth to every study that there is, whatever it is; even your badminton can have new ideas or else it must close.'
'I really do take a very firm – not firm in the autocratic sense or authoritarian sense – but a firm intellectual and academic position. And they reach for this, they really reach for this: whereas I've seen and observed, and I've even tried it myself obviously, but it doesn't work the other way. The idea that you can park the kids and they can play in a crèche, and your husband can go up there and have a pint, and you can go do a bit of painting – it seems to me that people don't really want that,

*they can do those things in their home; what they want to do it seems to
me is to get away from their environment, get out of it, and get into
something which is demanding, which is exciting really.'*

A specifically *Teaching* role is often felt to have a stronger claim on
the adult educator than *Recreational* or *Participatory* or *Community*
activities:

*'What had been going for years was that we were jamming them in and
saying 'paint'. The teacher and an assistant went round cooing or
grunting and everyone was very happy; it was a nice social group. But I
didn't feel that this was what we are about. One of our priorities is to
improve the quality of what's going on in educational terms, and I think
that a lot of the teaching that goes on in craft subjects is of the very worst
kind. . . . We recognise the importance of human relationships and the
social component . . . and we have to try to improve the teaching
without completely destroying these good things.'*

*'Now I don't believe we're in the business of community development.
Maybe I've changed over the years, maybe I've refined my thinking, or
maybe I've still got a very long way to go. I think that we can contribute
an educational role which will give assistance in this business of
community development, that we ought to limit ourselves to that which
we can do.'*

Lastly, a refreshing example of the confidence in the value of their
work which can be generated in adult educators by the concern for
quality in teaching:

*'I think our biggest bugbear is fitting in untrained teachers from
university – or has been in the past.*
They don't turn up at any training courses?
*No, no, they're far too superior! It does worry me actually, and I get a
lot of complaints back from students. I think many of them are unaware
that teaching standards have risen an awful lot. We still get the person
from university who turns up and says, "Oh, I've been through that",
and he thinks he's doing us a favour turning out. And yet I can go down
to a woodwork class and the way the class has been really thought
through from the students' point of view is absolutely astonishing, and
the way it's been prepared. We do seem to be set I think on some sort of
collision course if something isn't done because students are reacting
very unfavourably, increasingly unfavourably to this approach. And
I've never had so many direct complaints about tutors as I've had this
year.*
They complain they're just being lectured at, do they?
*That's right, they're dull. "Haven't they ever heard that there's
something else besides chalk', they'll say. I've been very fascinated by
this. I think one of the reasons why is that many of our students who
come to academic courses are also in a language course, and it seems to
me there's been a real revolution in language teaching. I'm very*

fortunate in that I've got a couple of very forward-looking tutors who have trained themselves and are slowly training the others, as I said previously, to make an integrated scheme. And what I find now is that if you get students who've had experience of that sort of teaching and are then put in rows and talked at, they can see that it's not fruitful. Also I think it represents some sort of change in attitude towards universities. I think people used to be deferential but I think universities have lost that status in society and the deference is no longer there.'

The spare-time adult educator

So far no direct reference has been made to the values and attitudes of the spare-time adult educator. Yet they merit separate attention, for they are bound to be different from those of the full-time worker: the spare-timer's career is committed elsewhere and he is, therefore, much less affected by the feelings of insecurity which condition the attitudes of his full-time colleagues. Generally, he has neither the time nor the opportunity for anything like their engagement in creative experiment; in recognition of this the initiative in new areas of work will often be taken by senior officers:

'I've tended to get involved in certain specialist areas, especially provision for the handicapped, which is something that's interested me, and I've tended to do this from the centre – provision for the mentally handicapped, physically handicapped, lip reading, braille, and one or two other things, and then once the thing is launched the centre's encouraged to get on with it. But I think one problem with (spare-time) principals is that the amount of time they've got for this sort of development, involving liaison with Social Services and suchlike, is so limited that you just can't really expect it, so you've got to set this up yourself.'

The attitude of the spare-timer is most likely to be conservationist – keeping things going will often be as much as he can do.

Time and opportunity are not the only constraints making for a conservationist attitude. As they are still typically paid by results, that is by the number of classes or by student enrolments, they would be putting their income at risk if they neglected what is traditionally supported by students in order to experiment: ' It stifles organisers' initiative – they're far too concerned with getting the last class off the ground when perhaps they would be better spending their time looking at developing some other areas.'

We do not wish to suggest that the spare-time centre heads' sole or even prime motivation is to maximise their incomes – only that there are significant pressures related to income and time in their situation which do not encourage an exploratory attitude. In this context it was suggested in Chapter 4 that the financial reward is unlikely to be the only motivation for the spare-timer, ' . . . he may to some extent be a volunteer'; interviews frequently supported this view:

'We are very poorly paid, it is a labour of love.'
'I don't think anyone does it for the money, I certainly don't.'
'Every September I say I'll never do this job again – I must be crackers.'
'I'm loath to pack it up because I enjoy it so much.'

The differences in attitude between spare-timers and full-timers are best brought out not by quotations from interviews but by the findings of the questionnaire. From this two sharply contrasting groups were drawn, one of 133 full-time adult educators in the larger Specialised Institutions (Sp. 1 and 2) and one of 186 spare-time practitioners in small Specialised Institutions (Sp. 3 and 4). The appropriate question was introduced in this way:

'If we are asked, as we sometimes are, to justify the expenditure of public money upon non-vocational adult education we usually do this by citing some of the many functions it performs. Here is a mixed dozen of some of the functions which are often cited in this way:

1. *helping us to develop physical fitness and maintain health;*
2. *remedying the deficiencies of those with inadequate previous education;*
3. *developing a sense of community involvement;*
4. *developing creative and artistic enjoyment and skills;*
5. *promoting social contacts and combating loneliness;*
6. *compensating for the frustrations of routine and undemanding work;*
7. *passing on traditional skills and a cultural heritage;*
8. *helping us to adapt to rapid technological and social change;*
9. *providing recreation in our increasing leisure;*
10. *developing critical and intellectual interests and abilities;*
11. *offering compensatory opportunities to the physically and socially disadvantaged;*
12. *raising standards of personal and household care.'*

(These have been numbered for ease of reference but were not numbered in the questionnaire though they were presented in the same order.)

The respondent was then asked the following:

*'Please put a **tick** against up to four of these which seem to you to present the most convincing case for public expenditure. Please put a **cross** against up to four of these which seem to you to present the least convincing case for public expenditure. This is a difficult question; if you find it an impossible one simply leave the boxes **blank**.'*

Of the 319 questionnaires in the group with which we are now dealing only fourteen were in fact not filled in. Scoring was done by simply adding the pluses (ticks) and the minuses (crosses) for each item, so that the resultant score might be itself a plus or a minus. In Table 9.1 these scores have been reduced to a base of one hundred for ease of comparison.

Table 9.1   Attitudes of full-time and spare-time adult educators

Full-time (133)		Spare-time (186)	
Rank order of functions	Score	Rank order of functions	Score
2	+62	4	+56
11	+52	9	+53
10	+38	5	+47
5	+38	2	+29
4	+35	3	+14
3	+14	6	+ 8
6	+ 4	11	+ 4
7	— 4	10	+ 3
8	—13	7	+ 1
9	—16	1	— 1
1	—24	8	—32
12	—39	12	—33

The spare-timers put at the top of their list the arts and crafts (4), followed closely by recreation (9) and social contacts (5), there is then a gap before we come to remedying educational inadequacies (2); intellectual interests (10) and work for the disadvantaged (11) come quite low on the list. There is no hesitation in putting forward an entirely traditional curriculum including a prominent social and recreational element. In contrast, work for the two categories of disadvantaged groups (2 and 11) is at the top of the full-timers' list, followed (after a gap) by intellectual interests (10), social contacts (5) and the arts and crafts (4). Recreation (9) is near the bottom of the list.

It would appear therefore that the spare-time adult educator has no hesitation in acknowledging his *Recreational* view of the service. In contrast the full-timer knows the political value of stressing work of a *Compensatory* kind in arguing a case for public expenditure.

Chapter 10

Adult education 1976-77: a threatened service?

The last few years have been a period of economies and cuts in adult as in other fields of education. We wanted to try to make some estimate of the effects of these cuts and particularly of their effect upon enrolments. All enquiries of this kind return in the end to one source of evidence: Form 109 FE. Stats. which all Local Education Authorities should complete and return to the Department of Education and Science in November each year. Since this form provides the basis not only for our figures but also for the national statistics of adult education published each year in *Statistics of Education* its nature and its limitations deserve some attention.

Form 109 FE. Stats. is a return of 'all students enrolled as at 1 November' in 'courses and individual classes supervised by a paid instructor' and held in 'Adult Education Centres, Evening Institutes, Other Further Education Centres, Youth Clubs, Community Centres, etc.' It is a return of numbers of individual students, not of enrolments: 'each student should be counted once only regardless of the number of classes attended'.

The inadequacies of this as a record and a measure of participation in adult education are well known. (The whole matter of the collection of statistics is, in fact, under review by the Department of Education and Science.) The main ones are:

1. It excludes non-vocational students in Colleges of Further Education and other major establishments, and may thus exclude as much as a quarter or more of the total student body.
2. It excludes all students who enrol after the beginning of November. This may not have been a large number in far-off days when most students enrolled for three-term courses. It is certainly a very large number now, when so many short courses begin later in the session.
3. Even within one authority and even over a short period there can be surprising changes in the amount of information provided and in the ways in which it is categorised and presented. This makes comparisons between authorities, and even comparisons from year to year within one authority, hazardous and at times impossible.
4. It is much easier to count enrolments than to count individual students, and since the request for this information comes at a busy time in the session it is not surprising that some heads of centre take the easier course.

5. Not all authorities always make the return.

In spite of these difficulties Form 109 had to be used as best we could. So, as a last request to long-suffering Local Education Authorities, we wrote in December 1976 asking for (*a*) copies of Form 109 FE. Stats. for November 1975 and 1976, and (*b*) information, if it were readily available, concerning changes in fees and regulations. Replies were received from seventy-four authorities, and these yielded fifty-six sets of complete and comparable forms; they comprised twenty-five non-metropolitan counties, seventeen metropolitan districts, twelve London and two Welsh authorities. We decided to measure provision not by the total number of students but by the number age twenty-one and over. This seemed a more relevant and reliable figure than the total number of students recorded on the Form since this (*a*) includes provision for younger age groups and for Youth Clubs with which we had not, in the rest of the enquiry, been concerned, and (*b*) has a built-in decrement caused by the excision from the form, over these three years, first of the under fifteen and then of the under sixteen age groups. Calculated on this basis eleven authorities had over 20,000 students (twenty-one plus, November 1976) fifteen had between 10,000 and 20,000, nineteen had between 5,000 and 10,000 and eleven had under 5,000. So they seemed reasonably well distributed by size as well as by type.

Numbers of students

A comparison of the number of students age twenty-one plus recorded by these fifty-six authorities during the last two sessions showed a decrease of about 8 per cent between 1975 and 1976. This figure is given to the nearest whole number only and further detail is omitted because we consider it unreliable in two ways.

(a) The omission of provision by Colleges of Further Education. One can only guess at the effect of this, but since Colleges of Further Education tend to be relatively stable institutions with considerable resources they might well be able to cushion the effects of economies more easily than other institutions. If this were so then a survey which omits them will tend to err a little in the direction of pessimism.

(b) On the other hand there is the fact that in all enquiries of this kind the recipients who respond tend to be those who are interested in and well disposed towards the subject of the enquiry. So the authorities who responded to our enquiry and were able to send us the information requested were likely to be those who were interested in and on the whole well disposed towards adult education. They form a self-selected and therefore unrepresentative sample of authorities as a whole and conclusions based upon their evidence alone are bound to err considerably in the direction of optimism.

Fortunately, it was possible to check this finding against statistics being collected by a group of H.M. Inspectors. These were based upon a larger sample of authorities and (more important) one which was not, as ours was, self-selected – though it also omitted Colleges of Further Education. We already knew that our figure would, on balance, err in the direction of optimism; this second set of data gave us some idea of the probable amount of error as well as confirming its direction. Taking all this into account our best guess (and it can be no more than that) is that the number of students age twenty-one plus in Local Education Authority institutions probably fell by about 11 per cent between 1975–76 and 1976–77. We believe this to be a conservative estimate and shall comment upon its significance later.

There is no significant correlation, as we thought there might have been, between amount of provision and ability to withstand economies: as Table 10.1 shows, the large authorities (in terms of adult education provision) fare as well or as ill as the small ones.

Table 10.1   Students, twenty-one plus: Gains and losses 1975–76 to 1976–77

No. of students	Authorities gaining	Authorities losing
Over 20,000	2	9
10,000–20,000	5	10
5,000–10,000	7	12
Under 5,000	2	9

What is clear is that the range of variance between authorities is very wide, ranging from a gain of 26·3 per cent to a loss of 71·1 per cent. So how you fare as an adult student still depends to an enormous extent upon where you live.

Fees and regulations

Information about changes in fees and regulations was presented in many different ways so that returns from different authorities were very frequently not comparable. But there were sixty-three replies which could be codified, and the general picture which they gave is as follows:

There was evidently a very common assumption in 1976 that an increase in students' fees of about one-third was 'normal' and 'in line with national policy'; it is often justified as 'keeping up with inflation' and with the rise in tutors' fees in particular, and there is frequent reference to the recommended fee increase of 30 per cent contained in the DES's circular 14/75. Of these sixty-three authorities, forty expressed views of this kind and did in fact keep their fee increases below 33⅓ per cent. Of the other twenty-three authorities twenty increased fees by amounts ranging from 40 per cent to 75 per cent. The three remaining authorities imposed increases of 150 per cent to 500 per cent, two of them in an attempt to raise fees to a level at which they would cover total costs (i.e. costs of administration, accommodation, etc. as well as costs of teaching). The normal range of fees resulting is shown in Table 10.2.

Table 10.2 Percentage increase and levels of fees 1975–76 to 1976–77

Percentage increase	Range of fees per term (£)
Up to 33⅓	1.50–4.00
40 to 75	2.50–6.00
150	c. 5.00
200 to 500	c. 9.00

Information about concessionary fees was less complete: in most returns they were not directly mentioned, which should perhaps be interpreted as meaning that they had not been increased. But many of them will have risen as normal fees have risen, since they are calculated as a proportion of these. Specific mention of increases was made by seventeen authorities and applied mainly to pensioners. In most cases the increase was small, but in five cases half the normal fee was being charged and in three cases the full fee (with of course, the possibility of remission to those in need).

Many authorities have sought to postpone or lessen the shock of fee increases by reducing instead the amount of tuition which the fee buys. Thus the length of term is frequently reduced from twelve to ten or even eight weeks, and the duration of a class meeting from two to one and a half hours. There seems to be a general conviction that this is more easily tolerated than a sharp rise in fees, and no doubt this has been found to be so. In fact, of course, changes of this kind constitute in themselves a sharp rise in fees. Thus if a fee is raised from £2 to £3 students are being charge 50 per cent more. But if the fee is held at £2 while the term is reduced from twelve weeks to eight and the class period from two hours to one and a half they are being charged 100 per cent more. And if the fee is raised as well, the increase goes up to 200 per cent. So the devices which are intended to soften the blow may in fact worsen its consequences.

A third way of increasing fee income is to raise the average enrolment per class and most adult educators, given a choice, will prefer to do this rather than to raise fees. Similarly, the increasing use of averaging or of net budgeting schemes encourages the promotion of large classes in order to compensate for small ones or to raise funds for other purposes. So there is certainly a general tendency to increase the profitability of classes by increasing their size, although we cannot quantify this.

Fees and student numbers

Fees are raised by direct or indirect means, and the number of students falls. Fifty-one authorities sent us data which enabled us to see if there was any connection between these two facts. Certainly there seems to be a correlation between the amount of the rise in the one and the amount of the fall in the other, as Table 10.3 shows:

Table 10.3   Fees and student numbers 1975–76 to 1976–77

Percentage rise in Fees	No. of authorities showing rise in students 21+	No. of authorities showing fall in students 21+	Student numbers 21+ av. percentage change
33⅓ and under	14	17	— 4:8
40–75	2	15	—13:2
150	—	1	—19:8
200	—	1	—49:6
500	—	1	—71:1

But the connection is not necessarily a causal one. Increases in fees are so often associated with cuts in adult education budgets and other restrictions on provision that it is difficult to prove that the fall in the number of students is caused by one factor and not by another. The probability is that it is caused by the combination of many factors, but the presumption that fee increases are important among these seems a reasonable one and one that is supported by the evidence. Perhaps the most significant thing in the table is not the obviously catastrophic effect of the few very large fee increases but the difference in effect of increases of up to 33⅓ per cent and those of 40 per cent to 75 per cent. In actual fees the difference is between a range of £1.50 to £4.00 and a range of £2.50 to £6.00 per term, yet this can have an effect upon recruitment which, though less dramatic than the figures at the bottom of the table, may in the long run be more damaging since it affects a much larger proportion of the population.

Conclusions

A decline in the number of adult students of 11 per cent in one year may seem not untoward in present economic circumstances, and not in itself a disaster. This, however, is to underestimate the long-term effects of such a development and (equally important) of the methods by which it has been brought about and the shifts in attitudes and expectations which have accompanied it.

1. The decline has to be seen against a background in which growth, not stasis, is the norm. The demand for adult education has been rising in the last two decades as the direct and inescapable result of the preceding growth and extension of initial education; it is still rising and will continue to do so. So the number of frustrated potential students is far higher than this figure of 11 per cent suggests, and the educational loss is

far greater. One authority – not a large one – and one which had actually increased, not decreased, its provision – writes of the bitter experience, of 'having to turn away over 2,000 students', and many echo this.

2. Reductions in length of course and of class meeting do not only, as has been shown, increase the cost to students; they also decrease the amount of teaching and learning that goes on. This is as absolute a loss as is the loss of students. So we ought to be asking how the amount of tuition given, as well as the number of students enrolled, has declined. To measure this a record of student-hours would be needed, and this does not exist. But it is not difficult to envisage the sort of picture that it might give. If the number of students drops by 11 per cent and if the amount of tuition which their fees buy were found on average to have dropped by 20 per cent (not an unreasonable figure) the loss in student-hours would be about 30 per cent. It may be that this is our situation; that in one year the amount of tuition given by our adult education system may have been cut by nearly one-third.

3. The process seems likely to go on and may even accelerate in 1977–78. The Department of Education and Science has already, in circular 1/77 of 14 January, recommended yet further increases in students' fees, and most authorities seem to think that their financial problems in the 1977–78 session will be at least as great and probably greater than those of the 1976–77 session. If they are, then adult education will no doubt again find itself suffering cuts which are proportionately much larger than those imposed upon other educational services. Some are already talking of a further 40 per cent increase in fees.

4. Increases in the size of classes and reductions in the length of courses have educational as well as financial consequences, though little attention seems to be paid to them. A class of twenty-five or thirty is no doubt a heartening sight for a county treasurer or a head of centre or even for an over-anxious teacher, but it is not likely to benefit the student. For him it means a diminution of opportunity of personal contact with the teacher and a dilution of tuition. Nor is a short course necessarily a good thing in itself. It is true that we have adhered too long and too unthinkingly to the two-hours-a-week-for-two-or-three-terms formula and that innovative adult educators have broken away from this to experiment, profitably, with shorter and more varied course structures. But there is also a need, in most subjects, for courses which permit sustained practice and study over at least two terms and often for much longer. Without a solid core of work at this level there is a danger that we may be offering our students a varied succession of *hors d'oeuvre* but rarely a nourishing meal. And nothing is more demoralising for teachers than to have a programme which is a series of beginnings – except, presumably, to have no programme at all.

5. The notion that students' fees should cover teaching costs is now a common assumption. The danger is that when a position like this is established it becomes very difficult to retreat from it: what begins as an emergency measure becomes a principle which nobody questions. Yet this is a new principle and it represents a radical change in policy. Until comparatively recently adult education was, in this country, regarded as part of the public educational system to be maintained by public funds; to be sure, a fee was charged, but it was more in the nature of a registration fee than a substantial contribution to costs, and there was concern that it should not be set at a level which would discourage the poorer members of the community from using the service. This was an element in our educational system of which we could be proud and which colleagues in other countries admired and envied. It is now being destroyed. Over considerable parts of the country adult education is now regarded not as part of the public educational system but as an optional extra which those who want must pay for, and which is available only to those who can pay; the role of the educational service becomes that of the provider of accommodation and some administrative support for self-financing leisure activities. It is not melodramatic to describe this as a radical change in educational policy; the surprising thing is that it has gone on largely unremarked and, in the main unopposed. Among adult educators the general feeling seems, quite understandably, to be one of helplessness; most of our interviewees felt that all they could do was to make the best of a bad job and protect their students as best they could.

6. Fees rise and the number of students falls; probably over 150,000 students were lost to adult education in 1976. Who were they? Upon this the opinion of adult educators is pretty well unanimous: those who are lost tend to be those who are below average in income, in education and in social confidence. There are no national statistics to support this but there is plenty of evidence at local level: area officers see that the loss of students is greater in the poorer than in the well-to-do parts of their area and the heads of centres cite the falling off of enrolments from council housing estates: 'When fees go up there is often a slight increase of enrolments in the better-off places. I think the impression must be that if it costs more it must be better. But it has a disastrous effect in the industrial areas.'

'We're approaching a point now I think when pay limits are really beginning to bite, and this coincides with the time when holidays are over and children are having to be fitted out for school . . . and the ladies in our classes are going to be asked to find £5 for a term. They're going to decide which they choose: is it to be food for the family, clothes for the children or their own education fee.'
'This is the first year that they've really tackled me quite ferociously and said: "Look, if we want to come to a dressmaking class we've not only

got to pay the fee; we've got to pay our fare to get here, find a baby sitter, buy our material – we just can't do it any longer". And this is only £3 a term. If it goes up to £5 next year, as is proposed, that really will be the death of the kind of adult education that we think we can provide and ought to provide in an area like this.'

Or, as seen from county and city hall rather than from the adult education centres themselves:

'There has been a marked fall in enrolments in rural areas this year, particularly in areas where salaries are on the whole lower.'
'There has been a total collapse of rural evening classes.'
'Higher fees produce lower enrolments, higher staff–student ratios, a greater proportion of concessionary students, inability to experiment with new classes or diversify provision.'

7. There is of course a real and widespread concern among adult educators for work with 'disadvantaged' groups (the old, the unemployed, the physically and mentally handicapped, the institutionalised, illiterates, immigrants, etc.), and a strong resolve to maintain this work despite all economic difficulties: 'This is our lifeline and we must keep hold of it whatever happens.' Local Education Authorities share this concern, encourage such work, and admit disadvantaged students to courses at much reduced fees or at no fee at all. But mainstream adult education often suffers as a result:

'Work with the disadvantaged is developed at the expense of our general provision.'
'The money for literacy work is mainly found from general adult education funds.'
'The additional income from increased fees all goes to finance work with the disadvantaged.'
'Mainstream work has been cut to provide funds for literacy work and for work with socially deprived mothers.'

Most adult educators accept this diversion of funds as justified and inevitable in present circumstances, but the very high cost of much of this work with disadvantaged groups is beginning to raise doubts: 'If you put on something special for a handicapped group it may cost you as much as, say, five ordinary classes. But it's much easier to get that through than to get funds for even one or two normal classes.'

In fact special provision for the identifiably and conspicuously disadvantaged does little to offset the socially and educationally discriminatory effects of increases in fees. Indeed, it may be strengthening those effects by diverting funds from mainstream adult education and creating a system in which you have an elite group paying high fees, a disadvantaged group paying no fees or very low fees, and nothing much in between. But those who suffer from the discriminatory effects of high fees are not in the main those to whom the label 'disadvantaged' is attached. They are the very much larger group of men and women with minimum education, low wages, young families, no established habit of attending adult classes and no claim to special provision or concessionary fees. To reach into this great middle mass of the population has always been the adult educator's most challenging and yet most rewarding task, and the current concern for the more conspicuously disadvantaged may prove to be a diversion from it.

8. Perhaps the most lasting effect of current fee and enrolment policies will be their effect upon the recruitment of the adult educators who still have to make their careers and who will carry the service up to the end of the century and beyond. What young man of ability and spirit will now choose adult education as the field which can best use his talents and reward his endeavours?

9. The final irony is that this progressive and probably irreversible impoverishment of the adult education service may turn out to be pointless, for it may not even succeed in making the minor savings that are its aim. The well-to-do areas will accept higher fees, will cover costs and may even show a profit. But over many other parts of the country it is becoming apparent that there is a point at which increased charges become counter-productive. There are already areas – and there will be more in session 1977-78 – in which the proportion of costs recovered from fees and in some cases the actual income from fees is less than it was before fees were raised. So policies which were intended to be thrifty may turn out to have been financially profligate; they were always, of course, educationally profligate, for they were prepared, without thought, to waste and disperse the educational capital and goodwill accumulated by many generations of adult teachers and students.

Chapter 11

Conclusion

This chapter consists in part of conclusions based on evidence which can be marshalled and in part of impressions which are the product of many hours of talking with adult educators. To have continually repeated such phrases as 'it seems to us that' or 'our impressions is that' would have been tedious. But they are, of course, to be understood throughout.

Adult educators

1. Adult educators are on the whole deeply and personally committed to the service of adult education. A consequence is that they tend to overwork themselves and to be overworked. This tendency can be found in all types of institutional setting and among spare-time, part-time and full-time practitioners.
2. A conflicting impression but one which is equally strong is of a lack of confidence, a sense of insecurity and a desire for public approval. This arises from a rational, not a neurotic, appraisal of their situation.
3. Most full-time and some part-time adult educators feel that their role is essentially an innovative and creative one, and value highly the responsibilities and the satisfactions which this brings.
4. Commitment and creativity of this order is possible only to the full-time or substantial part-time adult educator; it is not possible to the normal spare-time adult educator nor would it be reasonable to expect it of him. To a considerable extent, then, the health and development of the adult education service depends upon the number and quality of its full-time or nearly full-time workers.
5. Even to the full-timer creativity and commitment are possible only if his conditions of employment give him a wide degree of autonomy and enable him to make his own choices and decisions, his own experiments and mistakes.
6. Institutions and the administrative framework within which they work differ markedly in the degree of autonomy which they provide for the adult educator.
7. There are other limitations upon autonomy than institutional ones. Lack of sufficient administrative and clerical support is one which

is found at all levels of the service. This may result in a sense of perpetual conflict between administrative and educational demands or, partiularly in the case of spare-timers, a resigned acceptance of administrative and clerical tasks as their main function.

8. Equally inefficient is the inflexible imposition of regulations (concerning such matters as enrolment, fees and attendance) which are centrally determined and which often do not seem to have much regard for the conditions in which they are to be applied. We have been astonished to find how often decisions on such matters are taken without any effective consultation with the people mainly concerned. This seems an antiquated mode of management. The inevitable response to it, and the only way of retaining some slight measure of flexibility and local control, is the long and demeaning tradition of what is politely called 'respectable deviousness'. The enrolment requirements imposed by some authorities are so high that, if strictly observed, they would make experiment impossible and prevent any work with minority groups.

9. Any scheme of averaging or of net budgeting which releases the adult educator from such controls and which enhances local autonomy is to be welcomed. But most such schemes have not been running long enough for all their consequences to be apparent, and we see possible difficulties as well as obvious benefits. They may encourage the development of over-large classes as well as of small minority groups, and they may divert the energies of the adult educator from educational to fund raising activities. And the more successful he is in these the easier it may be for his budget to be reduced.

10. More diffuse in its influence, but perhaps most important of all to the adult educator, is the generally supportive or dismissive attitude of the authority towards adult education, for this attitude will soon spread throughout the education service and will therefore colour his relations with all his colleagues. A supportive attitude usually shows itself in the appointment of a senior officer with adult education as a major responsibility.

Types of institution

11. A major division is between specialised adult education institutions and non-specialised or multi-purpose institutions.

12. Within multi-purpose institutions the major differences are those determined by the nature of the host institution. In most cases this will be either a College of Further Education or a Secondary School; it may also be a Leisure Centre, but examples of this are at present very few.

13. Although type of institution is an important variable it is not a

decisive one, for adult education institutions (and adult educators) tend to be highly idiosyncratic. So the ranges of variance within each type are very wide indeed. Moreover, within each type one can find enterprising institutions with high standards and unenterprising institutions with low standards; the adoption of a particular institutional type is not in itself a guarantee either of success or of failure.

14. The demographic environment of an institution we found to be a less important factor than we had expected. Indeed it is important chiefly in the negative sense that a certain minimum catchment population is necessary if certain minority activities are to be possible at all. Since an adult education institution normally deals with only a very small sector of its total catchment population it can determine what that sector shall be. So, consciously or unconsciously, it selects its own environment.

15. Staffing seems to us the most important factor of all. Institutional patterns and the administrative framework which enclose them seem to us good or bad in so far as they can attract and keep able adult educators and in so far as they can ensure for them a wide measure of autonomy. They are, of course, unlikely to do the first if they cannot do the second.

16. How effective even a good staff can be is determined by the general level of an authority's expenditure upon adult education. This is always a very small proportion of its total educational expenditure, but even so it varies very widely indeed (from almost nil to over 2½ per cent) between one authority and another. So what kind of adult education service you get and how much you have to pay for it depends upon where you live.

17. Specialised Institutions seem to provide for the adult educator the greatest degree of autonomy, and in the few which have some teaching accommodation of their own this was even more obvious; even quite modest premises of his own can considerably enlarge the range of initiative open to an adult educator and increase his confidence.

18. In multi-purpose institutions autonomy must always be limited by the fact that the adult educator is not the person ultimately responsible for adult education policy and development. In practice this structural loss of autonomy may be mitigated in various ways.

19. No matter what kind of institution may be providing it, most adult education takes place in school accommodation out of school hours. Where adult education is based on either a Specialised Institution or a College of Further Education such accommodation is borrowed; where a school is the host institution the adult educator shares it. Such joint use of premises is bound to produce friction, but we expected that this would be less for the sharer than for the borrower. We found, however, that this was not generally the case. Perhaps the expectations and demands of sharers are

greater or, more probably, the conventions of sharing may not be as clearly established and understood as those of borrowing, so that the sharer is less certain where he stands.

20. In all multi-purpose institutions the fact that policy is not in the ultimate control of the adult educator is likely to create some feeling of insecurity, and the fact that adult education is part of an institution whose main purpose lies elsewhere is likely to create some feeling of marginality.

21. As a host institution for adult education the College of Further Education seems to have certain inbuilt advantages:
    (a) Adult education is statutorily part of further education and is financed from the same budget.
    (b) Students in further education are closer to adult students than are school children both in age and in the part-time and voluntary nature of many of their courses.
    (c) Colleges of Further Education, like adult education institutions but unlike schools, are accustomed to seeking out students from among their catchment population and planning courses to fit them.
    (d) They have a tradition of departmental independence which can mitigate the structural loss of autonomy for adult education.
    (e) They are accustomed to, and staffed for, a three-session day.

22. These are potential advantages only; they may not be realised. Many, perhaps most Colleges of Further Education, particularly those in the large cities, are fully employed in technical and vocational education and have little or no time for or interest in adult education. The potential advantages are likely to be realised only in those colleges, mainly in smaller and more scattered centres of population, which have been given or have developed a clear commitment to the education of the adult community as a whole. This is usually expressed through the establishment of a Department of Adult Education, and the size of this is an important factor; it will not be felt to be and treated as an established part of the college unless it makes a substantial contribution to the total of student-hours.

23. It is here that the barriers between vocational and non-vocational education, deplored by many adult educators, are most likely to be broken down and that a more integrated system of continuing education is most likely to develop.

24. The school as a base for adult education has one obvious advantage: its ubiquity; it can provide accommodation for adult education in small communities and with little capital expenditure. This can be done, and has traditionally been done, simply by allowing a specialised adult education service to use school premises after school hours. Increasingly, however, it is done by making the school the host institution for a combined school, youth and adult service and so creating the kind of multi-purpose institution which

is customarily called a Community School or College.

25. As a host institution for adult education the school seems to have certain inbuilt disadvantages:
    (a) There is a wide age gap between school and adult students.
    (b) School education is compulsory and full-time, adult education is voluntary and part-time; there are wide organisational and attitudinal differences between the two services.
    (c) The school tradition tends to be one of central control rather than departmental independence.
    (d) The school–youth–adult integration excludes Further and Higher Education, the very sectors of education with which adult education is likely to have most in common.

26. The Community School is, of course, an attempt to remake the school in a new image not just to make a new kind of multi-purpose institution. As this goes on and as a new kind of school emerges some of these disadvantages will diminish or disappear. But some are, as far as one can see, structural and not easily remedied.

27. Local authorities could ease some of the practical problems inside the Community School by more realistic staffing and depreciation arrangements – some of the operating difficulties are not necessarily inherent in the school situation.

28. We found less evidence of continuity between the different fields of work of the Community School than we expected. Co-operation between youth services and adult education seemed no more effective than that found in many other situations, and less effective than that found in some joint adult and youth services. And the amount of adult participation in school classes seemed, in practice, surprisingly small. On reflection it seems to us inherently unlikely that any substantial number of adults will be able to conform to school timetables or will find school courses apt to their needs.

29. Community Schools are dedicated to the education of the whole community; their members of staff sometimes have contracts which express that commitment and are in theory community educators. In practice only a few key members of staff seemed to us fully to accept this role; most tended, not unnaturally, to relapse into the role in which they felt most at ease, most confident and most skilled: they became once more school teachers or youth workers or adult educators. It may be that there is an inevitable time lag here, and that we shall not see the Community School fully developed until its staff is community trained.

30. It is not for us to make judgments about schools, but we must record our impression that this community setting, this openness to the world outside the school, can be a very good thing for the school. So it is not surprising that we sometimes had the impression that the community work was valued mostly for the indirect contribution which it made to the life of the school – which, after

all, is bound to be the main concern of the institution as a whole.

31. The linking of adult education with youth service in joint adult and youth systems might be thought to be a natural and a relatively easy one. In practice it can present many difficulties, and the general opinion among the adult educators to whom we spoke seemed to be opposed to the integration of the two services. Nevertheless the sharing of premises and staff can yield practical benefits. Within adult and youth services we again noticed that, as with Community Schools, the genuine commitment to the joint role felt by key members of the service was not shared by all. There was the same natural tendency to relapse into that role – youth worker or adult educator – which was supported by experience and training. Perhaps compromises of this kind either here or in Community Schools are in practice no bad thing.

32. On all counts the Specialised Institution with its own premises seems to provide the best base for adult education. It is often argued that, whatever its virtues, such an institution can only be educationally and economically justified in large centres of population. We doubt this. It seems to us that any reasonably coherent population of 25,000 or so could use fully and support a Specialised Institution with modest premises of its own and a full-time adult educator with adequate administrative and clerical support. This would cost little or no more than the provision of equivalent accommodation in a multi-purpose institution – the return educationally and socially would be far greater.

Ideas and programmes

33. Although there are marked differences in curriculum between different types of institution there is also a surprising consistency in the provision of a common core curriculum in institutions of all types. The impression is of a broad national consensus about what kinds of things adult education ought to offer, but we do not know what the processes are which determine and maintain this consensus or what the channels are through which they operate.

34. Different concepts of the function of adult education co-exist in most institutions, but with different emphases. Thus the larger Specialised Institutions and Colleges of Further Education seem much concerned with *Teaching* and *Compensation*, the rural Community Schools with *Participation* and *Recreation* and the Adult and Youth organisations with *Compensation* and *Recreation*. All, but especially of course the Community Schools, would claim a concern with *Community*.

35. Innovative capacity was most clearly shown in the larger Specialised Institutions, followed by those Colleges of Further Education in which adult education had departmental status. Adult and Youth

organisations and the urban Community Schools also showed a high innovative capacity, but in more restricted fields. The smaller, mainly rural, Specialised Institutions and the also mainly rural Community Schools are, as their environments would lead us to expect, the least innovative institutions – though as is to be expected Community Schools with their part-time and full-time staff show more initiatives than do the rural Specialised Institutions with their mainly spare-time staff.

36. Though student participation in the running of centres is widespread we heard more stories of failure than of success in attempts to set up responsible student organisations or committees. Nor was there as much enthusiasm for this among adult educators as we had expected to find, and many claimed that students' interest was limited to social affairs and to their own activity or class. There was also a fairly strong feeling among adult educators that the influence of students upon, for example, programme planning would be likely to be conservative and unadventurous, that they would tend to like and to try to maintain what they are accustomed to and enjoy; we found some evidence that this was indeed the case. The most developed student organisations tend to be found in Specialised Institutions – particularly those with their own premises – and in Community Schools.

37. Clubs and societies are found in most institutions whether they have formal schemes of affiliation or not, and are increasingly used as a substitute for classes which adult educators no longer have the means to provide. But since Community Schools attach such importance to *Participation* as an end in itself they tend to value clubs and societies highly, often more highly than classes; they sometimes outnumber classes and form the main element in a programme. We see their value, although the number of people who do actually participate in the running of a club or society must be a quite small proportion of its total membership. But if an institution develops clubs and societies at the expense of classes and learning groups it must surely dilute and dissipate its educational influence.

38. Work with disadvantaged groups is clearly a matter of great concern to adult educators and is well developed in all types of urban institution; clearly such groups will be more difficult to establish in scattered rural communities. We could not but admire the zeal and enthusiasm which adult educators bring to this work. But it is not and is not likely to be numerically a major part of total adult education provision and its importance is sometimes overestimated – though for reasons that are understandable.

39. There is only one word which we have heard even more frequently than 'disadvantaged' and that is 'community'. We are not proposing to attempt the impossible task of defining it, but note some of the implications of 'community education' a term which is very widely

used, and not by any means only by adult educators in explicitly-styled 'community' institutions. It carries the implication of a new start, a reaching out to people not normally touched by adult education, a questioning of traditional forms and subjects, an attempt to break through the boundaries of the institution to a wider range of local contacts. This may seem vague but it is invigorating and is felt to be so; it produces a sense of freedom and of release from academic traditions and inhibitions from which new and more firmly focussed initiatives will surely come.

The current situation

40. We have no doubt at all that adult education is indeed under threat and that in some parts of the country its very continuance is in doubt. A new principle, that adult education should be a self-supporting leisure activity for those who can afford it, is replacing the old principle that adult education should be part of the publicly funded educational service. This is a shift in policy in some authorities which has encountered little organised criticism or opposition and may therefore prove to be irreversible.

41. Cuts and economies which are much more stringent than those imposed upon any other sort of the educational service have necessitated steep fee increases, and these have already resulted in the loss of large numbers of potential students. It is, as always, the poor and the less well educated who tend to be excluded. There is a real danger that adult education may split into two segments: a heavily subsidised compensatory service for the conspicuously disadvantaged and an unsubsidised, and therefore highly priced, leisure service for the well off.

42. To these wounds adult educators add their own self-inflicted ones. They have too readily accepted the absurd assumption that adult education, with its miniscule staff and resources, can be expected to make good all the failures of initial schooling. And they have been too prone to minimise, indeed to disregard, their own not inconsiderable achievements in this respect – for even as long ago as 1969 and without any special provision or funding 42 per cent of students in Local Education Authority classes had a terminal age of education of fifteen or less (NIAE, *Adequacy of Provision*, 1970). This is no justification for complacency, but it is also no justification for the disabling feelings of failure and guilt from which too many adult educators seem to suffer.

43. In such a situation it is not surprising that so many adult educators should speak of their work with the disadvantaged as a 'lifeline'. It satisfies both their humanitarian impulses and their need for the public approval and support which they feel is denied to their normal work. In these circumstances adult educators need the

disadvantaged as much as the disadvantaged need adult educators.

44. Such humanitarian and egalitarian impulses have always been an essential part of adult education, although different generations of adult educators express them in different ways and direct them into different channels. Adult educators would not be adult educators if they were not driven by such feelings. But adult educators would also not be adult educators unless they were also driven by a strong concern for teaching, for the extension of teaching and for the improvement of teaching. Both sets of values are necessary to the health of the movement. They are of course opposed, but the conflict and tension between them is a creative one; it is this which gives adult education its special character and its drive. The adult educator has not to reconcile them but to hold them in balance and to enable both to operate. This is far from easy and it produces, as we have seen, conflicts and tensions in the adult educator himself. But it is the essence of his task.

Appendix A: Adult education and the sociology of organisations

It has been our intention as far as possible to avoid using pre-existing theory in writing this report though as the work progressed we became increasingly conscious of the relevance of certain concepts used by students of the Sociology of Organisations. The influence of these will have been apparent to the reader versed in such theory and as a postscript it seemed appropriate to more formally demonstrate the connection. What follows is not intended as a comprehensive demonstration of the relevance of particular theoretical concepts to adult education for such an exercise would lie outside the scope of this report; it is a guide to where the interested reader might begin to develop his understanding. Given this purpose the number of references is small. Most of the readings will be concerned with other than adult education organisations but this is inevitable given the limited application of theory of this kind to that field.

Organisation

As used by sociologists the term organisation implies a complex structure based on a hierarchy of control, extensive division of labour and staff specialisation. By comparison, adult education organisations are typically 'simple' with few staff, often only one, and limited division of labour, though there will be a hierarchy of control either within the complex structure of a Community School or College of Further Education or within the broader framework of the Local Education Authority's Department of Education.

As normally understood this concept would appear, therefore, to have rather limited application in adult education. The reader interested enough to assess the relevance for himself would find Etzioni (1964), Chapter 1, a very useful introduction.

Boundary and social networks

An effective starting point here for the adult educator is an article by Musgrave (1973). Having made the point that organisational boundaries are rarely geographical he observes (p.170):

'Possibly because the term "boundary" has been applied in an unthinking and reified manner little attention has been given to the problematic nature of organisational boundaries. In particular it has been forgotten that boundaries do not exist "out there" in society, but are perceptions in the minds of those filling positions in and interacting with those in the organisations concerned. Once this is realised it is clear that those concerned may hold differing perceptions of where any organisation's boundaries lie. . . . Because service organisations are by definition dealing with personal problems conflict over defining organisational boundaries would seem probable.'

Such conflicts over perceptions of boundaries are inevitable in adult education given the problematic nature of such concepts and issues as community education, the status of practitioners, the sharing or borrowing relationship with other institutions, the voluntary nature of student participation and the role of students in decision making. In the latter area practitioners may have a diferent perception of the appropriate degree of student involvement in decision making from the students themselves. Again adult educators seem, in general, to see programme planning as their responsibility though it is possible that the policy of the authority expresses another view. If we see such a stance as an attempt by the practitioner to establish a boundary then one of the functions of boundary definition is apparent – it can be seen as an attempt by organisational members to ensure that dependence on the support of 'outsiders' (students) does not interfere detrimentally with the work of the institution.

In a multi-purpose institution a headmaster/principal may have a different perception of adult education from that held by the person immediately responsible for the programme; such an institution may be seen in terms of the 'college as community' whereas the adult educator may feel it more appropriate to operate 'out there' in the community. School or college staff attitudes expressed in references to 'my room', 'my equipment' are probably best understood in terms of boundaries of influence. In trying to develop a community role a practitioner may find himself in conflict with the concept of organisational boundary held by another institution – is it social work or adult education?

Musgrave (p. 178) concludes, '. . . that those who advocate community schools or deschooling or any other similar structural change in the school system must, if they wish to be successful, base their strategy upon the characteristics of the organisation that they want to change as well as those of the structure that they wish to create and upon the social networks in which the school is set and with which it interacts.' This introduces the important concept of *social networks*.

It is clear from the diaries which they kept, and from interviews, that adult educators in different kinds of institution operate within *social networks* which show marked differences in terms of the dominant groups involved. Thus in Specialised Institutions the dominant social network of full-time staff consists of other adult educators, that is other heads of centre, responsible officers, and teachers of adults. In contrast Community Schools (Comm. 1) have a network dominated by local clubs and societies and Adult and Youth organisations have a highly developed range of contacts with youth groups and voluntary organisations. Such differences are not only an expression of the conceptual view of adult education held by institutions but also provide important reinforcement for such a view. Any attempt to change fundamentally the kind of service which a particular type of institution offers will do well to analyse the existing social networks and to determine those likely to be most appropriate to the new role.

Such an analysis may lead, for example, to an awareness of the need for structural changes or adjustments in the method of providing the service. The range of possible initiatives is very wide: it might be thought appropriate to detach a worker from the centre and place him 'out there', or it may be decided to locate a much larger proportion of programme activities away from the centre in village halls, homes for the elderly, community centres, etc. The need to develop new social networks, to cope with what for many is a new function, is well illustrated by the literacy programme; contacts with personnel officers in industry, social welfare agencies, voluntary tutors, remedial teachers, etc., seem to be essential to such work.

Of particular importance to adult education is the need to establish appropriate contacts with minority groups. In the school context McDowell (1973) has argued that '. . . it is minority groups who have most to gain from an adaptive and responsive school system, and most to lose from a rigid and centrally controlled system in which their interests and values are under-represented at every level and with which they have few effective contacts.' He concludes that 'the first priority in creating an adaptive and responsive school system is to *increase the autonomy of the school in relation to its purpose.*' The relevance of such a view to adult education is apparent: where practitioners in Specialised Institutions have been given a large measure of autonomy they show a remarkable capacity to experiment and to operate an adaptive and responsive system.

Deppe (1969) has developed the concept of boundary to look specifically at the adult educator as a *boundary definer.* He sees the boundary definer as 'dealing with the flow and counterflow of forces between an institution and its environment', in such a way 'as to make the boundary either more or less permeable to the forces that inhere in the interaction between organisation and environment' (p. 119). In this role the adult educator applies his own hierarchy of values and priorities, that is in so far as organisational policies and resources permit him to do so. He '. . . is capable not only of ignoring, accepting, modifying, mobilizing, or otherwise responding to forces that exist, but is also likely to generate or create forces that might not have existed without him' (p. 120).

Talking to adult educators has demonstrated for us the relevance of both concepts, boundary and boundary definer. The practitioner often has considerable freedom to define the appropriateness for the service of particular needs or demands, to decide that a particular idea or activity is relevant to his function. Again, some are highly creative in relation to their environments others are highly passive. The best expression of passivity came from the practitioner who when asked if his programme provided for any kind of disadvantaged group or individual replied, 'I have never had any requests'; this contrasts sharply with such observations as 'I see myself as a catalyst for developing the ideas of others' or, 'I pride myself and I get my kicks out of being creative.'

Goal

In defining and redefining boundary the practitioner is often engaged in *goal definition and redefinition*; what business are we in? is a question which frequently engages adult educators. Here the lack of goal definition and the social networks within which he operates render the practitioner very vulnerable. Clark (1958) suggested in a seminal essay almost twenty years ago that in adult education there was an 'uncommon . . . degree of goal ambiguity' (p. 3) which rendered practitioners highly susceptible to external influences. As a result they were 'highly situation-directed and relatively little goal-directed', with 'student choice determining the evolution of his curriculum' (pp. 7, 10). Elsewhere he developed this theme (Clark, 1956) suggesting that in any organisation members try to justify their objectives by reference to values. He goes on to observe that values are likely to be precarious if they are not defined, when those who implement them have positions which are not fully legitimised, and when they are not acceptable to a 'host population' (pp. 328–9).

There can be little doubt, as Clark observed, that adult educators have great difficulty in defining their goals (a notoriously intractable problem in education generally) and that the values which they express are often not acceptable, particularly in multi-purpose institutions, a situation where, in addition, their prestige is not established. Again, the broader 'host population', in the shape of local authorities, often appears unsympathetic to the services' goals and values by making severe economies and by imposing a restrictive regulatory framework.

Student power in goal determination expressed through participation in programme planning is a particularly problematic area. The report findings show that in the main both heads of centre and senior officers are wary of the consequences of such student involvement. In the broader but closely related area of community participation Hill (1972) (p. 99) has commented that,

'The concepts of "community" and "participation" are both highly ambiguous; the combination of circumstances in which both local authorities and middle-class-dominated pressure groups are very ready to present themselves as spokesmen for 'the community', and, on the other hand, deprived groups are slow to organise and find it difficult to penetrate the corridors of power, create a situation in which the ostensible goals of community participation policies are continually under threat and could be subverted almost without the fact being noticed.'

The relevance of his arguments would not be lost on adult educators; indeed the reader is likely to find Hill (Ch. 5) a generally rewarding reference.

Community

The above reference to community is a reminder both of the currency of this concept and of its ambiguity. However relevant it may be in adult education the report has demonstrated the difficulty of using the term in any precise way. Space precludes a detailed treatment here and the reader is referred to Musgrave (op. cit.), and the references there provided.

Innovation

Adult education is, despite recent economies, at least in some authorities, an adaptive and responsive service, searching out new tasks and redefining existing ones; in our view an effective service has to have this capacity for innovative response. Innovation, and the appropriate organisational setting for its successful implementation, are topics which have produced much research activity and copious published material in recent years. We have suggested that some institutions, with appropriate staffing, have more innovative capacity than others, maintaining that individual and environmental characteristics are probably less important than organisational ones.

The reader is likely to be confused by the mass of available material in this field, even by the growing volume of published findings relating specifically to education. An appropriate starting point might be Baldridge and Deal (1975) (particularly Ch. 7). A relatively short summary of relevant ideas is contained in Baldridge and Burnham (1975).

Role and role conflict

In looking at the responses of adult educators to their jobs the concepts of role and role conflict were implicit in much of our thinking. Our enquiries did not uncover any consensus about role conflicts arising out of joint adult/school or college teaching appointments. There is, however, considerable inter-role conflict between the demands of the work situation and those of the marriage partner/parent role. The former not only often requires long, unsocial hours but also frequently intrudes into the home. For many the literacy programme has made the problem more acute because in order to provide a necessary element of accessibility and privacy for potential students the head of centre has often publicised his own phone number as a first contact point. In this way the leisure time of the adult educator is not protected from the intrusions of the work role (if it ever was).

Probably a more important area of conflict is reflected in the often expressed frustrations which result from an awareness of a gap between what the practitioner believes to be a desirable and appropriate provision and what policies, finance and administrative demands on his time permit him to do. This might be conceived of as a difference between a *professional* interpretation of the role and what is administratively possible. The use of the term professional is not, however, very helpful unless it is clearly defined and traditional approaches at definition have led Millerson (1964) to conclude that '. . . few seem to be able to agree on the real determinants of professional status'. If the reader is anxious to achieve an understanding of the concept Millerson would be an appropriate starting point particularly if read in association with a more recent publication by Johnson (1972). Attempts have been made, though not very sucessfully, to relate the concept to adult education in this country (*Adult Education*, September 1961).

A comprehensive essay on role and role conflict was contributed by Burnham to a collection of readings edited by Baron and Taylor (1969) (Ch. 5). For the beginner this is a most useful introduction and it might be supplemented by reading an excellent little book by an adult educator – Ruddock (1969).

Bureaucracy

The often tight framework of rules and regulations within which adult educators work can be conceived of as an aspect of *bureaucracy*; like the term professional this is a much used but often ill-defined concept. It is frequently suggested that there is a fundamental conflict between *bureaucratic standards* and *professional norms*. There can be no doubt that many adult educators find that regulations clash with their view of what the service should be about. Therefore an understanding of the nature of this conflict would appear to be appropriate and here again Etzioni (1964), Chapter 8, is an effective starting point.

Front-line organisations

There have been many references to the autonomy of the adult educator in the Specialised Institution. A particularly appropriate concept here is that of *front line* organisation the characteristics of which are as follows: 'Organisational initiative is located in front line units. Each unit performs its task independently of other units. There are obstacles to the direct supervision of the activities of such units.'[Dorothy Smith, quoted in Gilbert Smith (1970)]

These characteristics are present to some degree in all specialised adult education institutions. They are physically separated from their 'bosses', indeed practitioners typically claim that in effect they do not have a 'boss'; organisational initiative lies with them. They run their own programmes and are subject to little, if any, direct supervision; the attempt to supervise through regulations is often effectively circumvented. Front line is a very useful concept when comparing the situations of practitioners in Specialised Institutions with those in multi-purpose institutions. In the latter the 'boss' is present in the institution and more direct supervision is possible – regulations, therefore, seem to press harder.

Gilbert Smith (op. cit.), particularly Chapters 5, 8 and 11, is very useful here. Indeed he is likely to provide a useful introduction for any reader to whom many of the concepts referred to are new and who has difficulty in seeing their relevance for the study of particular organisations; he is concerned not only to explain basic concepts but also to demonstrate their relevance to, for example, schools, voluntary organisations and prisons.

References

Adult Education (September 1961) Vol. XXXIV, 'On professional standing', The Report of a Study Group.

Baldridge, J. V. and Burnham, R. S. (June 1975) 'Organisational innovations: Individual, organisational and environmental impacts', *Administrative Science Quarterly*, Vol. 20.

Baldridge, J. V. and Deal, T. E. (1975) *Managing Change in Educational Organisations*, California.

Baron, G. and Taylor, W. (1969) *Educational Administration and the Social Sciences*, London.

Clark, Burton R. (1956) 'Organisational adaptation and precarious values: a case study', *American Sociological Review*, **21**, pp. 327–36.

Clark, Burton R. (1958) *The Marginality of Adult Education*, Boston.

Deppe, Donald A. (October 1969) 'The adult educator: Marginal man and boundary definer', *Adult Leadership*, **18**, No. 4, pp. 119–30.

Etzioni, A. (1964) *Modern Organisations*, New Jersey.

Hill, M. J. (1972) *The Sociology of Public Administration*, London.

Johnson, T. J. (1972) *Professions and Power*, London.

McDowell, D. (1973) 'Some organisational issues in the education of minorities', *London Educational Review*, **2**, No. 1, Spring, pp. 37–42.

Millerson, G. (1964) *The Qualifying Associations*, London.
Musgrave, P. W. (1973) 'The relationship between school and community: A reconsideration', *Community Development Journal*, **8**, No. 3, pp. 167–78.
Ruddock, Ralph. (1969) *Roles and Relationships*, London.
Smith, G. (1970) *Social Work and the Sociology of Organisations*, London.

Appendix B: Head of centre interview schedule

Background

Yourself
1. Please tell me something about yourself, e.g. name, age, qualifications, your career with dates, how you see your career developing.

Your Job
2. Please tell me something about your job, e.g. its title, what you do.

Your Centre
3. Please tell me something about your centre, e.g. location, availability, size, staff and the nature of their appointments (title, time commitment).

Running your centre

4. Whom do you see as your boss or bosses? How is this responsibility demonstrated?
5. What problems, if any, do you encounter in your work?
6. What part, if any, do you (*a*) students, and (*b*) teachers, play in the running of your centre?
   What part do you think they should play?
7. What have been the main lines of development of your centre during the last few years and what developments would you like to see in the next few years?
8. Tell me something about your current programme.
   In what way does it differ from last year's?
   How did any new activities arise?
   What did not enrol adequately?
   What (if anything) do you most regret losing?
   What activities are not shown in your published programme?
9. On what aspects of your work, if any, would you
   (a) like to be able to spend more time?
   (b) like to receive further training?
10. In providing adult education Local Education Authorities tend to work through one of three main types of institution:
    (a) the independent centre or group of centres;

(b) the Community School or College;

(c) the College of Further Education or Technical College.

Which of these do you think likely to be most effective?

11. Other things being equal, which kind of job would you prefer?

(a) full-time adult education;

(b) adult education plus youth service;

(c) adult education plus school or college teaching or counselling.

12. Is there anything unique or special about your centre or its neighbourhood?

13. It seems possible that non-vocational adult education may be forced to become financially self-supporting. If this were so, what long-term effects do you think it would have?

Appendix C: Examples of classification by course titles

Most courses can readily be assigned to the appropriate category, and examples are given below. But there is a small number of borderline cases (though not enough to invalidate general conclusions) and examples of these are also given. Sometimes additional evidence (perhaps an explanatory note in the programme) will solve the problem. Courses which still remained in doubt were divided between the two contending categories.

1. *Craft and Aesthetic Skills*

1.1 Courses related mainly to personal care and the household economy, e.g. Beauty Culture, Car maintenance, Cookery, Dressmaking, Flower Arrangement, Gardening, Soft Furnishing.
1.2 Courses related mainly to leisure time enjoyment, e.g. Carving and Sculpture, Drama, Drawing and Painting, Model Making, Music, Photography, Pottery.

2. *Physical Skills*

2.1 Courses related mainly to the maintenance of health and fitness, e.g. all types of Keep Fit, Keep Slim and Yoga.
2.2 Courses related mainly to leisure time enjoyment, e.g. all outdoor and active indoor games, sports and recreations including Dancing, Judo and Gymnastics.

3. *Intellectual and Cognitive Skills*

3.1 All language courses.
3.2 All other courses, e.g. Appreciation or History of Music or Drama etc., Archaeology, Bridge, Chess, Current Affairs, Genealogy, Psychology, Miscellaneous series of Lectures or Discussions.

4. *Courses addressed to Disadvantaged Groups*

For example The Elderly, Illiterates, Immigrants, the Unemployed, the Physically and Mentally Handicapped, Hospital Patients, Groups in Deprived Areas.

Borderlines

1.1 and 1.2 Embroidery? Woodwork? (mostly 1.1), Handicrafts and Mixed Crafts? (mostly 1.1).
1.2 and 2.2 Ballet?
2.1 and 2.2 Weight Training? (mostly 2.2).
3.1 and 3.2 German, French, etc. Studies?
3.2 and 4.0 Family or Marital Problems?

In allocating courses category 4 was given preference over all others so that any course, in any subject, which could be assigned to that category was so assigned.

Exclusions

All courses leading to an examination or a qualification were excluded, except those in which (as in some language courses) the examination was presented only as an option which some students might like to take up.

All separately financed courses for prisoners were excluded.

Index